Warning - Disclaimer

Freedive!

Dedications

To my mother who, from the first, encouraged me to
pursue the sport that I love.

To my wife Loren, whose patience, love and friendship
helped make this book possible.

David Sipperly

To my children, Michael, Loren and Marissa, with love.

Terry Maas

PHOTOS: LOREN MAAS (TAKEN WHILE FREEDIVING)

Freedive!

David Sipperly   Terry Maas

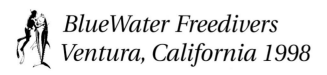BlueWater Freedivers
Ventura, California 1998

First printed April 1998
10 9 8 7 6 5 4 3 2 1

Library of Congress Catalog Number 97-78090
ISBN 0-9644966-1-5

CREDITS

Cover design and photos: Terry Maas
Book layout: Terry Maas
Line art: Chris Martinez 26, 28 ,40 ,41 ,42 ,43 ,48 ,49

Photography:
Gear chapter: A.B.Biller 52, 53, 55, 64; Ron Mullins 55; Seacure 56;
Body Glove 58; Xcell 58; Deep Thought 58, 61; Esclapez 59;
Debra Lipsett and Peter Mottur 53,54,55,59,60,62,63,65
Techniques chapter: Debra Lipsett 84 (U.R.I.), 87; all other photos and
video clips by Terry Maas
Photography chapter: Whale photographs (68, 96-97), obtained
under the provisions of NMFS research permit #882, copyright
Phil Colla/Hawaii Whale Research Foundation
Underwater hockey chapter: David Sipperly 111; all others by Terry Maas
Game gathering chapter: A.B. Biller 126; Riffe 126; Esclapez 126; Mares 126
Diving for depth records chapter: Jacques Mayol 134

*Editing: Beth Maas, Loren Sipperly, Suzanne Schlosberg, Susan Smith, Paul
and Janet Greenberg, Andrea J. Bernstein and Bart Ruebenson.*

Manufactured in South Korea on acid-free paper.

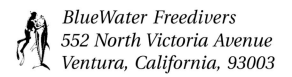

BlueWater Freedivers
552 North Victoria Avenue
Ventura, California, 93003

Acknowledgments

During the writing of this book, we relied on the input of established freediving experts to enrich the content. We would like to thank all the freedivers named in the individual chapters who contributed to this book.

The history chapter gave us the opportunity to study our freediving roots. It was a pleasure to have three divers who played such an important role in our modern freediving history share their experiences with us: Jack Prodonovich, Wally Potts and Art Pinder. Thanks to Dr. Samuel Miller for his passion documenting the history of diving, especially in the United States. His contributions and peer review were invaluable. To Bob Jackson for his historical books.

The two physiology chapters received review and/or contributions from numerous physicians, health-care professionals and physiologists. Our thanks to Andreas Agathos, M.D.; William Hurford, M.D.; Tom Millington, M.D.; Frank Farm, director of the Hyperbaric Treatment Center of the University of Hawaii School of Medicine; technical diving expert Bret Gilliam; and physiologists R.W. "Bill" Hamilton and Jacques H. Corriol.

The loan of gear and photographs from many diving manufacturers helped us illustrate a variety of quality diving equipment. You may refer to the captions, credits or Appendix—I for more information on how to contact the various contributors.

Terry's long-time friend and dive shop owner and instructor, Jerry Stugen, provided invaluable advice and encouragement for the chapter on freediving technique. To a large extent, we followed his training program, which he developed over 40 years while introducing novices to the sport. Bill Ernst, Beth Maas and members of David's freediving classes helped us present clear and concise illustrations of the various exercises and techniques introduced in the chapter. Thanks also to Jim Smith, owner of Ventura Dive and Sport, for the use of his pool facilities, to Stan's Skin Diving Shop for the loan of equipment and "kayak man" Mark Theobald.

Phil Colla and Skip Stubbs deserve special mention for their contributions to the photography chapter. Their enthusiastic, yet scholarly approach to the subject helped us put together a no-nonsense, information-rich introduction to the complex subject of underwater photography. Phil's photographs decorate many of the following pages. Over 95 percent of the photographs presented in the book were taken freediving. Only two photographs were taken while using scuba gear; both were of freedivers taken by professional photographer and award winner Jeff Rotman.

The hockey chapter sparkles with special contributions from Kendall Banks, Tim Burke, Carol Rose and the Central California hockey team, members of which generously donated a large portion of a morning workout to help illustrate the text.

We would like to thank the following contributors to the chapter on monofins: Peppo Biscarini, Mike Gower, Dietrich Lawrence, Chris Morgan, Glennon Gingo and Sonny Tanabe. Special thanks to Theresa Villa, whose words and image grace our pages, for making the concept of diving with monofins so appealing.

In appreciation for their assistance on the game gathering chapter, we'd like to thank the following champion spearfishers: Ron Mullins, Mike McGuire, John Murphy, Gerald Lim, Mark Barville and Greg Pickering.

The following individuals helped us research and illustrate the chapter on deep diving: Jacques Mayol, Jean-Jacques Mayol, Mehgan Heaney Grier and Francisco Ferreras.

As we sought information for this book, it became apparent that one non-profit organization, the Underwater Society of America, plays a large part in organizing and supporting freediving activities, namely fin swimming, underwater hockey and spearfishing. We thank the officers and members of the society for their continual support of freediving.

Our thanks, too, to Sherry Shaffer and Mike McGettigan who operate the ideal freedivng yacht, the Ambar III. Trips with Mike and Sherry have provided us with much of the raw material and photographs used to illustrate the text. Thanks also to John Ernst, Lee Somers, Ata Bilgili, Jim Hamilton and contributors to Mark Barville's Internet Freedive List and to Tom Pfleger and Tommy Rothery of the Polaris Supreme.

Contents

Manta rays, stallions of the seas.

Introduction

Freediving is a wonderful path to the underwater world that's easy on your pocketbook. Almost anyone who swims can learn this sport. For snorklers, just a breath and a kick begins the journey. What separates the well-trained freediver from the snorkler is that the freediver feels confident, serene—even euphoric—in water deeper than a few feet. This sport is so absorbing than an hour spent freediving erases a week of worries and tension.

Free to fly gracefully in any direction, freedivers experience a unique exhilaration. Their mental ease and special physiological adaptations make them feel as if they have no need to breathe—now or forever. It is narcotic. Peaceful.

The rewards of freediving are as varied as the activities you can enjoy underwater—sightseeing, photography, underwater hockey, mono-fin diving and game gathering. After we review the history of the sport, freediving physiology, gear and techniques, we'll explore each of the freediving specialities. We'll profile people just like yourself, who began this sport as "weekend warriors" and who, through enthusiasm and love for the sport, have become experts in their field. At the end of the book, you'll find a complete glossary of freediving terms and a reference for providers of freediving gear and services.

Humans share special diving adaptations with marine mammals. The most dramatic is the "mammalian diving reflex." Simply immersing your face in cold water causes a reflexive slowing of your heart rate. This, as well as other oxygen-sparing adaptations, helps to prolong your dives. With just a few weeks practice, you can develop your own latent freediving abilities.

While some people may dive deeper and longer, a 45-second dive to 30 feet (10 meters) puts you in the action. Since most of the ocean's color and animal life resides within 30 feet of the surface, there's little reason to go deeper. Forty-five seconds buys you enough time to gather game, take a photo or simply mingle as one with the fish. Best of all, the average person can master these dives in just two weeks without spending valuable travel dollars on gear. Your essentials—mask, snorkel, fins, wetsuit and weight belt— pack easily into a duffle bag.

You needn't be an athlete to enjoy freediving because the sport is more about mind-set, technique and correct weighting than strength. Your goal is to join the water, rolling with the gentle sea surface, never fighting it. When you learn the basic surface dive, you'll find that it takes very little energy to slip below the surface. Relaxed and confident, you choose the depth and duration of each dive. You'll be amazed how quickly your first 15-second dives become 30 seconds, 45 seconds—long enough to dive through 30 feet.

Trained freedivers experience an intense communion with their underwater world. Living in the moment, they see and feel what casual observers miss—the ocean's pulse, subtle changes in currents, apprehension in bait fish and a host of interactions among sea creatures. We've swum for hours with manta rays and whale sharks, come face-to-face with colorful sailfish and giant marlin. We've watched a pair of dolphins make love one minute then break off to single out and chase down a large jack for lunch.

Soft, smooth, quiet, confident, serene, peaceful: all of these adjectives hint at the intense pleasure well-trained freedivers feel. Imagine coasting below the waves, playing "pass the leaf" with wild dolphins, flying in formation with giant manta rays or simply joining a school of fish. Without a mechanical breathing apparatus, you're truly free—free to flow effortlessly into the womb-like, enveloping water, free to join the ocean not as an interloper but as a welcome friend.

You can compare the freediver to the glider pilot. Both enjoy an exhilarating world, silent of machinery, soaring like an eagle in the skies or gliding like a fish underwater. When the freediver takes a breath and descends, he's committed to returning to the surface again for air. Once the glider pilot releases his craft from the tow-plane, he's committed to continually planning for his landing. Without an engine, he can't go-around for another landing or reach a landing site outside his range. The freediver, like the glider pilot, must continually plan for the successful end of his dive—the pilot needs enough "air" to land, the freediver needs enough air to reach the surface.

You might ask, "Why freedive when all I need to do is strap on a tank and swim underwater for an hour?" Our answer is that freediving strikes a chord in those who enjoy a challenge—one that's free of the added attention required with scuba technology. Freediving is simple, unobtrusive and intimate. And there is a more primal reason why freediving feels so right: everyone of us has spent part of our life swimming in our mother's womb.

While freedivers make excellent scuba divers, the reverse does not necessarily follow—scuba-diving knowledge does not guarantee a successful freediving experience. In the 50s and 60s, when wide-scale scuba training became available, as a prerequisite to scuba training you had to demonstrate proficiency in freediving. Beginning in the 70s, the emphasis on "freediving first" diminished to the point that many scuba-training classes pay only lip service to the benefits of freediving.

Terry Maas' teammates John and Bill Ernst provide an excellent example of how well-trained freedivers make good scuba divers. In the late 60s, the brothers entered the National Scuba Championships in Monterey, California. While both were scuba certified, they had fewer than 10 tank dives each to their credit. They competed against others with thousands of scuba hours underwater. The Ernsts took an early commanding lead and never looked back. They attributed their spectacular win to the water skills they developed while freediving.

You've chosen an excellent time to begin freediving. The specialized gear you'll need—and there isn't much—is readily available and has been refined through decades of research. Interestingly, most of the best gear still comes from Europe, where the sport has flourished along the shores of the Mediterranean.

It is our intention to make this the finest guide to freediving ever published. We hope to enlighten you with the basics of the sport and entertain you with the riches of its varied specialties. We want to be clear, though; this book is not a "teach yourself," all-inclusive instruction book. No book on such a potentially dangerous endeavor can substitute for professional instruction. We insist that you enlist the aid of a competent instructor to guide you through basic freediving instruction.

Are there risks to freediving? You bet! Besides boat injuries, line tangles and sharks, you've got to be constantly aware of the possibility of shallow-water blackout—the results of simply holding your breath too long. Fortunately, good training in technique and physiology, plus a good dose of common sense, should keep you relatively safe.

In this book, co-authors David Sipperly and Terry Maas will be your hosts, guiding you through the exciting world of freediving. Combined we have over 60 years of experience. David, a two-time All-American Freediver, holds instructor credentials for a wide range of freediving and scuba classes, from basic training to instructor certification. Terry is four-time National Individual Skindiving Champion and spearfishing world-record holder. His book *BlueWater Hunting and Freediving* and his video *Bluewater Hunters* (produced by Laszlo Pal and viewed by over 25 million) have helped to introduce the sport to enthusiasts world-wide. From time to time throughout this book, we'll offer individual experiences when we'll refer to ourselves simply as "David" or "Terry." It is our sincere hope that you will find freediving as exciting and rewarding as we have.

Skin Diver Magazine began publishing in 1951 and for over a decade it focused on freediving issues. In the late 60s, its focus shifted to scuba diving. In the late 90s, the magazine again began to publish articles on the art of freediving.

PHOTO: FOOT AND SCHULLMAN

The primary interests of the first freedivers were spearfishing and game gathering. Art Pinder (left) and brother Don (far right) began freediving in the late 30s in the warm waters off Florida. They proudly display a jewfish they captured filming "Undersea Conquest," circa 1955.

PHOTO: LAMAR BOREN

California legends Jack Prodonovich (left) and Wally Potts, members of the "San Diego Bottom Scratchers," display an average day's catch at La Jolla Cove, San Diego in 1944.

Freediving history

Imagine shore dwellers foraging in tide pools for shells and fish, glimpsing the abundance beneath the shimmering blue water. Undaunted by cut feet, blurred vision and seawater-washed sinuses, a few souls ventured beyond the waves—into the belly of the Mother Sea to collect her promised riches.

The exact origins of breath-hold diving are unknown. Some archaeologists believe that Neanderthal man dived for food and depended equally on ocean resources and terrestrial resources—he hunted for shellfish as often as he gathered berries and nuts.

Freedivers appeared in widely separated civilizations along the shores of warm, clear seas. Aboriginal North Australian wall paintings depict men swimming with spears and strings of fish. The original inhabitants of the Bahamas were accomplished spearfishers and pearl divers.

South Pacific Islanders fashioned swimming fins from palm fronds and tar. They made diving masks from tortoise shells, which, when finely polished, became nearly transparent.

The first known case of occupational disease was caused by freediving. An article appearing in the March 1995 issue of the *National Geographic Magazine*, written by Bernardo Arriaza and Enrico Ferorelli, describes the life of the Chinchorro, a prehistoric tribe of fisherfolks who lived along the coast of Chile and Peru. Examination of the skulls of Chinchorrian mummies revealed that more than one-fifth (mostly males) exhibited bony masses protruding into their ear canals. The condition, now known as auditory exostosis, is common among people who dive in cold water without thermal protection.

By 4500 B.C., the Greeks and Romans had advanced the art of breath-hold diving to the point that they had developed lucrative businesses based upon the shells, pearls, sponges and food they gathered. Roman soldiers used sponges to carry fresh water supplies, to clean out wounds and to cushion heavy armor.

The Greeks used divers in naval warfare against the Persians. One story tells of a father-and-daughter team that swam over five miles through stormy seas and then dove to cut loose the moored fleet of Xerxes.

The Cretan civilization flourished in the Mediterranean around 1,500 B.C., spawning excellent fishermen and sailors who collected murex shells for their imperial purple dye long before the Phoenicians (1,200 to 700 B.C.). Their highly civilized society supported skilled artisans, many of whom were inspired by the sea. Their goblets and vases, decorated with paintings of lobsters, urchins, conch shells and octopuses, lead us to believe that the artists observed these creatures in their natural habitat.

Cretans believed in Glaucus, the diver god who symbolized both the lure of the deep and the songs of the waves. Greek mythology also refers to Glaucus as the most famous breath-hold diver. According to the Greeks, he was a fisherman who ate special seaweed that enabled him to dive for long periods of time. One day he entered the ocean but failed to return, and

This Peruvian ceramic vase, dating from the second century A.D., shows a diver wearing goggles and holding his catch.

thereafter became a god. Cretan legend tells of an ancient place where hero-divers, after swimming into the depths and searching for sea treasures, returned as divine individuals.

South Pacific pearl divers, working in depths over 100 feet, stayed underwater for up to four minutes. Attached to their canoes with a rope and ballasted by a heavy stone, they free-fell to the bottom. There they quickly filled a basket, also connected to the rope, with pearl shells. The divers ascended by pulling themselves up the line hand-over-hand. Climbing into their outrigger canoes, they proceeded to pull up their catch. They repeated the process many times throughout the day. Their basic equipment and techniques were so efficient that they are still practiced by native pearl divers and deep-water spearfishers.

Modern freediving began with the *ama* divers of Japan. These women, members of an elite diving organization formed in the 1800s, still practice their profession today. They begin diving as early as 11 or 12 years of age and may continue to dive into their sixties, usually diving half-naked in the cold waters of Japan. They make 60 to 90 dives a day, some as deep as 145 feet, to collect shellfish, seaweed and mollusks, which they place into nets they wear around their waists.

Ama divers hyperventilate for 10 to 15 seconds, taking rapid, deep breaths before taking a final deep breath—just short of full capacity. Japanese poets refer to their shrilled, pleasant hyperventilating sounds as "iso-nageki," the elegy of the sea. In the early 1930s, a Japanese exhibitor introduced goggles, made from two glass lenses glued into bamboo eye pockets, to the Europeans at the Great Exhibition in Barcelona. Today, they use modern masks but their profession is diminishing as young girls move to the cities to find other work. Currently, there are probably some 18,000 *ama* divers practicing their ancient techniques.

In early 1913, Greek diver Stotti Georghios retrieved an anchor from a remarkable depth of 200 feet (61 meters). Diving repeatedly to the wreck of the Regina Margherita, he used techniques that were very similar to those used by South Pacific pearl divers. Using a 100-pound rock for ballast, he descended feet first.

In the West, freedivers first appeared in Southern California. In 1929, Glen Orr logged his first dive. In 1933, the world's first continually active dive club—the San Diego Bottom Scratchers—was founded with 19 members, including Orr. Three widely known Bottom Scratchers include Jim Stewart from Scripps Oceanographic Institute, Jack Prodonovich and Wally Potts. Jack and Wally are featured in the television documentary "Blue Water Hunters." Jack is considered the inventor of the first diving mask in the United States and the underwater camera. Both Jack and Wally constructed the first spearguns in the United States and continue to actively coach others in the craft today.

To be considered for membership in the Bottom Scratchers, you had to harvest three abalones on a single breath-hold dive, catch a ten pound lobster, and wrestle a horn shark with your bare hands. New members removed the horn from the shark that they caught and placed it on the zipper of their swim trunks. As they swam along the bottom, the dangling horn would leave scratch marks in the sand, hence their name.

A few years later in the mid-1930s, a group of Europeans began exploring the French Riviera calling themselves "gogglers." This group included such now-famous divers as Hans Hass, Jacques Cousteau and American Guy Gilpatric.

In the upper left photo, Jack Prodonovich displays his gear.

Members of the San Diego Bottom Scratchers—affectionately known as the fathers of California freediving—made extensive use of paddleboards.
Above, Jack (left) and Wally Potts with white seabass. Left, Jack and Wally gather abalone.

PHOTOS: LAMAR BOREN

Guy Gilpatric, a popular writer for the *Saturday Evening Post*, brought the sport of freediving to the attention of westerners. From France he wrote, "I was unprepared for the breathtaking sensation of free flight which swimming with goggles gave me. It wasn't at all like flying a plane, when you are conscious of being borne by something tangible; there was a nightmare quality to this sensation as in a dream of falling, and in that instant I knew how Icarus felt when his wings melted off. I jerked my head out of the water and looked around to reassure myself. The bottom was 15 feet below me, now, but every pebble and blade of grass was distinct as though there was only air between."

Gilpatric captivated readers with stories of his "little band of serious sinkers" as they encountered the crafty octopus and the wary wrasse. His book, *The Compleat Goggler*, published in 1938, became the first definitive work on the sport. His writings drew together widely separated European enthusiasts and launched a sport that flourished along the shores of the Mediterranean until World War II.

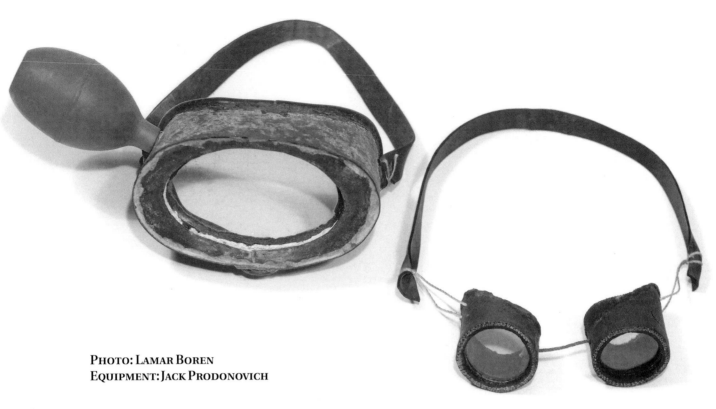

PHOTO: LAMAR BOREN
EQUIPMENT: JACK PRODONOVICH

Using the goggles on the right would cause the eyes of early divers to bulge painfully when they ventured into water deeper than 20 feet. Jack Prodonovich inserted a rubber bulb into the mask on the left to compensate for external pressures on the mask.

In view of today's standards of technique and gear, it's amazing that Guy's group grew. Without wetsuits, these early near-shore explorers could brave the temperate French waters only in the summer and then for just a few hours. Their nose-clips left sore, blue bruises and because of their habitual use of ear plugs, it's not certain if they ever equalized the painful pressure behind their ear drums.

Their precious goggles presented challenges to the user. About goggling for lintes fish in relatively deep water, Gilpatric wrote, "I blew out my air and went down the face of the cliff. The lintes were deeper than they looked, and below 30 feet the pressure was severe. I felt water forcing into my sinuses; the suction inside my goggles hurt my eyes, and though my ears were plugged, they felt as though twin tooth-aches had migrated north and settled there."

Because there was no internal way to equalize the pressure in their goggles against the increasing water pressure from outside, the goggles became painful to wear at 20 feet and temporarily deformed the eyeball at 40 feet—enough to cause visual distortions.

Guy called his group "sinkers" because of the way they commenced their dives. Their goal was to submerge without a splash. Because they wore no weights, they released the air in their lungs to help them descend. Using neither fins nor snorkels, they positioned themselves vertically in the water, head up. Then they exhaled and pulled themselves under with their arms. At about 10-feet deep they bent over and swam toward the bottom, usually carrying a King Neptune-looking, trident spear. They also believed that their empty chests gave them more mass with which to propel their hand-powered spears.

Like most early freedivers, Gilpatric was primarily interested in hunting game. He devoted much of his book to the frustrations and pleasures of hunting animals comfortable in their liquid world where he was, at best, a 50-second interloper. It's interesting to note that as his sport blossomed along coastal France, where legions of Europeans tromped down to the beach with their goggles and spears, Gilpatric began to notice a significant decline in the local fish populations. Perturbed, he found himself traveling

18

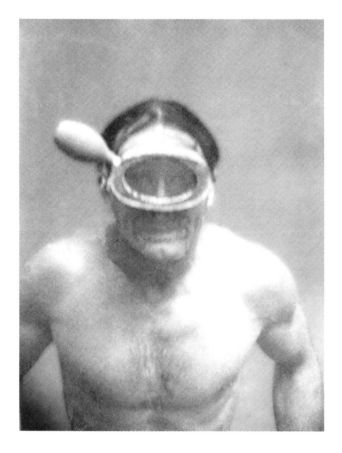

EQUIPMENT: JACK PRODONOVICH   PHOTOS: LAMAR BOREN

Jack Prodonovich surfaces (left) with a mask that does not yet include his nose. This 1945 photo was taken with Jack's first underwater camera. A later version of his mask (above) included the nose and sported corrective lenses. Note the ear-damaging earplugs.

farther afield for game. Like most true hunters, though, he had goals other than catching fish; on fishless days he remained enraptured by the excitement of the hunt and the unique environment. About such days, he wrote, "But always, by way of compensation, there is the gorgeous submarine scenery to look at and the kick of finding something new, strange and almost unbelievable."

Guy Gilpatric's peers suffered double vision, eye and ear pain and water intrusion into their noses and sinuses. Diving pioneers solved each one of these problems with progressive improvements to their gear. Unless gogglers aligned the two lenses on the same plane, they saw double.

The "monogoggle," made from a single lens of glass, eliminated the visual distortions. Because the design still left the nose uncovered, the mask compressed tightly onto the diver's face as he descended into deeper water.

The Japanese *ama* solved the pressure-equalization problem by the addition of twin air bladders that they piped into the mask. Instead of crushing the face, water pressure compressed the bladders, causing an air pressure injection into the mask—enough to equal the external water pressure.

In 1927 Jacques O'Marchal, a French goggler, developed and tested the first mask designed to include the nose. Covering the nose offered two major improvements: seawater was kept out of the nose and the diver could finally control "mask squeeze." By blowing air from their noses, divers balanced the external pressure on their masks with air pressure supplied from their lungs. In 1938, another Frenchman, Maxim Forjot, patented and commercially manufactured the first masks and snorkels.

In 1950, the Cressi Company of Italy developed the last major commercial improvement to the face mask: a compressible pouch covering the nose. For the first time, divers could clear their ears easily by sealing their noses during descent.

During the 1930s, inventive divers developed the last of the triad of essential freediving gear: the snorkel and fin. While both Leonardo Da Vinci and Ben Franklin drew imaginative swim-fins, it was the American entrepreneur Owen Churchill who introduced fins to the public, helping to popularize freediving. In 1938, while visiting Tahiti, Owen purchased a pair of swimming fins—crude models made of soft rubber and metal reinforcing strips.

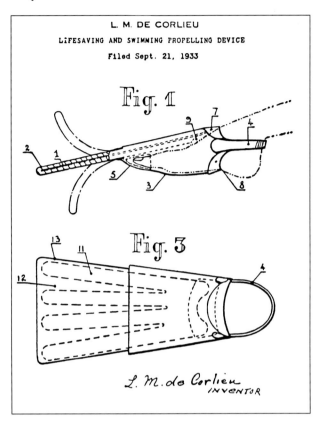

L. M. DE CORLIEU
LIFESAVING AND SWIMMING PROPELLING DEVICE
Filed Sept. 21, 1933

Fig. 1

Fig. 3

L. M. de Corlieu
INVENTOR

PHOTO: LAMAR BOREN

Owen Churchill (center), the developer of the "Churchill fin" stands proudly between Jack Prodonovich (left) and Wally Potts, circa 1950.

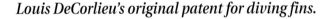

Louis DeCorlieu's original patent for diving fins.

Churchill's patent attorney discovered that another Frenchman, Louis DeCorlieu, had, in 1933, patented his so-called "swimming propellers"—an aid to swimmers on the surface. Owen contracted with DeCorlieu for the United States rights to his fins. At the same time, Churchill patented improvements to the fin; the most notable was the addition of tapering ribs that both improved support to the fin's tip and increased the fin's propulsion. With Owen's fins, the sport was elevated to new heights. His accomplishments are memorialized in the United States Freediving Championship Trophy, which bears his name.

Churchill made thousands of fins in his own plant and later licensed the Voit Rubber Co. to manufacture them. During World War II, both the Americans and the English purchased large quantities. Navy divers equipped with "Churchills" and covered in black oil gave rise to the name "frogman." First Swimaster, and later Voit developed their own "duck feet" models, very stiff, open-heeled fins that soon became the standard for both scuba and freedivers.

While we know Leonardo Da Vinci made drawings of underwater-surface breathing tubes, it's unclear who first patented the snorkel. However, it was the Frenchman Farjot who brought his "breathing tube for gogglers" into commercial production. The name "snorkel" was cast early after World War II because freedivers afloat on the surface with their backs awash resembled submarines with their snorkels (air tubes) extended.

With the problems of vision, propulsion and breathing solved, the last major advance—protection from the energy-sapping, mind-numbing cold—was mastered at the close of World War II. Woolen underwear, available at war-surplus stores, provided a brief transition in thermal protection before the wetsuit made its appearance in the 1950s.

While wool provided some protection against the cold, it stretched into a useless bag in the water. Divers solved the problem by wearing an extra swimming suit over the wool to keep the crotch in place. Electrical tape and rubber bands, wound barber-pole style around the extremities, prevented bunching and bagging. The complete ensemble included aviation headgear and special underwater demolition (UDT), rubber-soled, coral boots. Fully outfitted, a diver might enjoy 60 minutes in the summer and 15 minutes in winter before "freezing out."

In 1949, Dick Jappe (below, left) and Bill Wilcox display dry suits they made from patterns supplied by the Long Beach Neptunes dive club. Suits like these were quickly replaced by more efficient wetsuits introduced in 1951.

Like the other freedivers of this time, master spearfishing-gear maker and spearfisher Charlie Sturgill (above) used woolen clothing to extend his forays into cool Southern California waters, circa 1945.

In 1951 freediver Hugh Bradner, a California physics student, developed the theory of the "wet" suit. He reasoned that a thin layer of water, trapped above the skin by a tight fitting, insulated, stretchable material might keep the diver warm. His friend Willard Bascom suggested expanded neoprene.

Within six months, Bradner had developed a successful pattern. The Korean War was in full swing when the wetsuit came to the attention of famed underwater warrior Francis "Doug" Fane, who quickly recognized the strategic value of the design. Bradner formed a company named EDCO to manufacture the newly classified suits for the Navy.

By the 1950s books and magazines were filled with pictures and articles on freediving and spearfishing. *Skin Diver Magazine* began publishing in 1951. In 1953 the magazine announced "a new principle in frogman suits of elastically reinforced neoprene foam," and presented the EDCO suit for sale.

According to the May 1949 issue of *National Geographic*, an issue featuring the Bottom Scratchers, there were an estimated 8,000 freedivers in the United States. Like their predecessors, early-modern freedivers' primary goal was the pursuit of game—fish and shellfish. In 1950, Ralph Davis organized the

PHOTO: LAMAR BOREN

Unlike today when you have a myriad of freediving gear from which to choose, in 1940 when you wanted to freedive, you had to invent the gear. Probably America's greatest innovator of freediving gear was Jack Prodonovich. A somewhat older Jack demonstrates one of the first underwater cameras and pre-mask goggles he developed, circa 1940.

International Underwater Spearfishing Association. The organization held its first national freediving competition at Laguna Beach, California. Dimitri Rebikoff published his book, *Free Diving,* in 1956. It listed all of the dive clubs in the United States at that time—approximately 186. More than 120 of these were located in California.

Revolutionary "freediving fins" appeared in Europe early in the 1970s. The long-fin principle was designed by Pierre Buffa, who worked for the French company Sporasub. Terry Maas remembers his team's first look at the long, flimsy fins at the world-spearfishing championships in Spain. The strange looking fins made them laugh until they saw divers consistently diving 10 to 20 feet (4 to 8 meters) deeper than they had been able to four years earlier. After trading their flashlights for the new fins, the team returned to Malibu, where they tested the new long fins against their duck feet. Any member of the team equipped with the long, resilient European fins swam faster and longer than others using the stiff, stubby fins they were used to. Today's serious freedivers use these fins exclusively; many also use them when they scuba dive as well.

As freedivers, we owe much to our predecessors. You can find an excellent in-depth review of the contributions of the United States pioneers in *Last of the Bluewater Hunters* by Carlos Eyles. In his book, *The History of Underwater Exploration,* Robert F. Marx makes an excellent and comprehensive review of the world history of freediving. We'll discuss the history of particular freediving sports such as finswimming, depth records and underwater hockey in individual sections later in this book.

HISTORICAL FREEDIVING EVENTS

1910

1913 —— *Greek Stotti Georghios freedives to 200 feet (61 meters).*

1920

1927 —— *Frenchman Jacques O'Marchal tests the first face mask to include the nose.*
1929 —— *Californian Glen Orr logs his first freedive.*
1930
1933 —— *Frenchman Louis DeCorlieu patents the swim fins.*
San Diego Bottom Scratchers founded.
1934 —— *American Guy Gilpatric begins to write about freediving in the* Saturday Evening Post.

1938 —— *Frenchman Maxim Forjot patents and manufactures the first masks and snorkels.*
1940

1943 —— *Frenchmen Cousteau and Emile Gagnan successfully test scuba gear.*

1948 —— *First international spearfishing competition in Antibes.*
1950
—— *First United States spearfishing championships.* Skin Diver Magazine *begins publishing.*
1951 —— *Californian Hugh Bradner develops the wet suit.*

1954 —— *Great Britain invents underwater hockey.*

1960
1961 —— *South African bluewater hunter Tony Dicks lands a 317-pound black marlin freediving.*

1967 —— *Russians develop the first monofins in Siberia.*
1968 —— *Robert Croft dives to 231 feet (70 meters).*
1970
—— *Long freediving fins appear in Europe.*
1972 —— *The first European monofin competition.*

1976 —— *Jacques Mayol dives to 330 feet (100 meters).*

1980
—— *First underwater hockey world championships in Canada.*

Mikako Kotani swims gracefully with a wild
Atlantic spotted dolphin off the Bahamas.

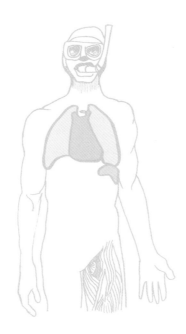

Physiology—part I

As a freediver, your most important asset is your own body. Treated with understanding and respect, your body will transport you to many wonderful adventures underwater. On the other hand, if you ignore the basic rules of physiology or fail to stay in shape, you may suffer serious injury—even death. Adding a dose of common sense to the knowledge you gain from this chapter should help avoid calamity. Although at times these two chapters may sound a bit morbid, keep in mind there are relatively few freediving accidents.

Each dive must be perfect. Once you descend, you're committing yourself to a successful journey back to the surface. Our job in *Physiology—part 1* is to help you understand the physiology of breath-holding and relate it to the inherent dangers of freediving. We'll start by addressing the mechanics of respiration, the gases of respiration, the human physiologic adaptations to breath-holding underwater and blackouts. In *Physiology—part 2*, we'll examine the direct effects of water pressure on your body and gear. This chapter ends with discussions of mental and physical stress, nutrition, heartburn and the effects of temperature.

RESPIRATION

Just as life begins and ends with a breath, so does a freedive. Breathing is such an integral part of life that we take it for granted, but freedivers can't afford to take such a casual approach to respiration.

Respiration is the exchange of gases—oxygen and carbon dioxide—between your lungs and the cells of your body. As you take a breath of fresh air, it warms as it journeys through your mouth and throat and into your lungs. In the lungs, air passes through an ever-smaller network of tubes to end in tiny grape-like sacs called alveoli. This is where the business of respiration takes place: oxygen is absorbed into the blood, and carbon dioxide exits the blood into the lungs. With a lining just one cell thick, the alveoli—all 300 million of them—when spread out would cover the area of a tennis court. In addition to collecting carbon dioxide and warmth, expired air picks up water and exits nearly 100-percent humidified. This is one reason why freedivers get cold and dehydrated.

The urge to breathe is caused primarily by high blood levels of carbon dioxide rather than low levels of oxygen. An increase in carbon dioxide causes a corresponding increase in blood-acid levels. Special cells in our brains, called chemoreceptors, monitor acid levels; they're so sensitive that they cause your breathing rate to double when carbon dioxide concentrations increase by just 3 percent. Other chemoreceptors, sensitive to oxygen, are located adjacent to large arteries; they monitor oxygen levels in your blood. Of secondary influence only, they do not stimulate breathing until oxygen levels fall well below normal.

Subconsciously, your respiration center controls both the rate and volume of your breathing so that the amount of carbon dioxide expired is the same amount you're producing in your tissues.

Fresh air entering the alveoli contains a higher concentration (partial pressure) of oxygen than the blood. Because gases move from a high partial pressure to a low partial pressure, oxygen diffuses from the lungs into the blood, helped by the rich capillary network (tiny blood vessels) bathing the alveoli. In the blood, oxygen attaches itself to the hemoglobin of red blood cells and travels throughout the body propelled by the force of your beating heart. At the tissue level (muscle, organs and brain), oxygen gets exchanged for carbon dioxide and water—the waste products of cell metabolism. These wastes make the return trip back to the lungs for removal.

> **The urge to breathe is caused primarily by high blood levels of carbon dioxide rather than low levels of oxygen.**

Increased ventilation is required to overcome snorkel-induced dead space. Dead space is that portion of your respiratory tract where gas exchange does not occur. To understand the seriousness of dead-space air, imagine breathing through a snorkel 20-feet long. After a short while you'd have to quit because all the fresh air would be gone and all you'd be doing is pushing used air back and forth.

In theory, the ideal lung would have no dead space; all the air in the lung would contribute to respiration. The air in your mouth and the breathing tubes leading into your lungs all contribute to dead space—about 2/3 cup of air (150 cubic centimeters).

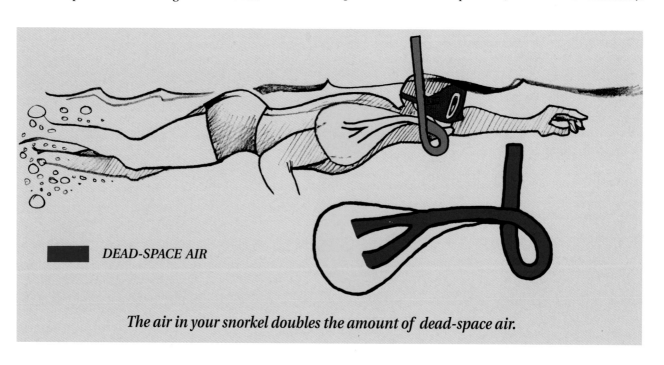

■ *DEAD-SPACE AIR*

The air in your snorkel doubles the amount of dead-space air.

Ventilation is the process that moves important gases in and out of your lungs. Freediving requires more efficient ventilation than land-based exercises because breath-holding and pressure changes both profoundly affect the essential gases of respiration—oxygen and carbon dioxide.

> **Increased ventilation is required to overcome snorkel-induced dead space.**

Your snorkel doubles your natural dead-space air volume. In order to move and dilute this dead-space air, divers must exchange large amounts of fresh air. Slow, deep respirations clear dead-space air more efficiently than rapid, shallow breaths.

Two muscle groups, the chest muscles and the diaphragm, contribute to ventilation. The diaphragm, shaped like a dome, separates your chest from your abdomen. Of the two muscle groups, the diaphragm has the greatest impact on ventilation; it is responsible for moving 75 percent of the air through your lungs.

During inhalation, the diaphragm contracts and descends into the abdominal cavity, increasing the volume of the thorax and lowering the pressure in the thorax; this draws air in. Exhalation is normally a passive process. During normal exhalation, the diaphragm and chest muscles return passively to their resting positions. However, during forced exhalation, the diaphragm is capable of pushing air out of the lungs with the help of the muscles lining the abdomen. At rest, the diaphragm may move up and down 1.5 centimeters. During deep breathing it will move 6 to 10 centimeters.

> *Proper breathing is essential for freediving. The best method of breathing primarily uses the abdominal muscles.*

Proper breathing techniques

For freediving, the best method of breathing primarily uses the abdominal muscles. This type of breathing is referred to variously as diaphragmatic, abdominal or Tai-Chi breathing. Notice how babies' bellies bulge outward when they sleep; they're using abdominal breathing.

In everyday life, the average sedentary person breathes minimally. Although they may feel fine, they're probably not providing enough oxygen for their maximum energy potential.

Without deep, abdominal-assisted breathing, you're left with only your upper chest muscles to move air and expel waste gases. Referred to as thoracic or chest breathing, this less efficient breathing pattern leaves air trapped in the lower portions of your lungs, where it stagnates. In thoracic breathing, the abdomen never relaxes enough for the free movement of the diaphragm. Without an abdominal-muscle assist, chest breathers rely on their upper chest muscles, which cannot deliver enough volume of air for anything but a sedentary lifestyle. In today's appearance-oriented society, women believe their waists aren't slim enough and suck their bellies in. Men, wanting to be macho, stick out their chests. Both actions create self-imposed strait jackets. Age compounds the problem. As you age, your chest wall loses flexibility.

As stress increases, so does reliance on chest breathing. In the water, this rapid, shallow and inefficient breathing cycle causes new divers to feel "out of breath." The result is frequently panic or exhaustion.

The ability to relax is one of the most important aspects of breath holding. A basic tenet of yoga states that if you control breath, you control life. To use relaxed abdominal breathing, take 10 to 12 breaths per minute without using your chest muscles. Jacques Mayol, the world freediving champion, is a master of yoga and meditation. Prior to his deep, breath-hold dives, he meditates, often using alternate nostril breathing—a method he feels builds energy, induces relaxation, heightens awareness and promotes creativity. We'll discuss the specific relaxation methods in the chapter on diving techniques.

HUMAN PHYSIOLOGIC ADAPTATIONS TO FREEDIVING

The human body is capable of remarkable adaptations to the underwater environment. Even an untrained diver will show a dramatic slowing of the heart when immersed. This is commonly referred to as the "diving reflex" or the "mammalian diving reflex"—one reason why most people can hold their breath longer underwater than they can on land.

> *The ability to relax is one of the most important aspects of breath holding.*

Immersing your face in cold water automatically causes the heart to slow. In the mid-1800s, physiologist Paul Bert first described this phenomenon in diving ducks. Later, the same mechanism was found to be common in diving mammals. Your heart slows gradually after immersion,

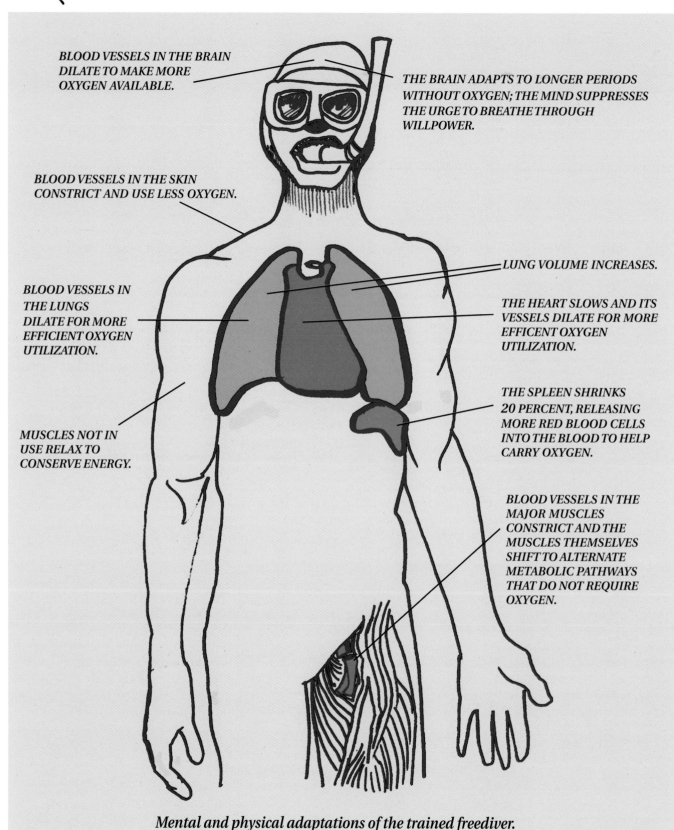

BLOOD VESSELS IN THE BRAIN DILATE TO MAKE MORE OXYGEN AVAILABLE.

THE BRAIN ADAPTS TO LONGER PERIODS WITHOUT OXYGEN; THE MIND SUPPRESSES THE URGE TO BREATHE THROUGH WILLPOWER.

BLOOD VESSELS IN THE SKIN CONSTRICT AND USE LESS OXYGEN.

LUNG VOLUME INCREASES.

BLOOD VESSELS IN THE LUNGS DILATE FOR MORE EFFICIENT OXYGEN UTILIZATION.

THE HEART SLOWS AND ITS VESSELS DILATE FOR MORE EFFICENT OXYGEN UTILIZATION.

THE SPLEEN SHRINKS 20 PERCENT, RELEASING MORE RED BLOOD CELLS INTO THE BLOOD TO HELP CARRY OXYGEN.

MUSCLES NOT IN USE RELAX TO CONSERVE ENERGY.

BLOOD VESSELS IN THE MAJOR MUSCLES CONSTRICT AND THE MUSCLES THEMSELVES SHIFT TO ALTERNATE METABOLIC PATHWAYS THAT DO NOT REQUIRE OXYGEN.

Mental and physical adaptations of the trained freediver.

and after 30 seconds your pulse rate may fall to 50 percent of normal.

Before the start of freediving competitions, David Sipperly splashes cold water on his face to help induce his mammalian diving reflex. This act reduces his heart rate, prepares him for the heat of competition and slows his heart for his first dive.

Record-setting deep scuba divers Bret Gilliam and the late Sheck Exley have taken advantage of this reflex as well. In his book *Deep Diving,* Gilliam describes pre-dive procedures for his record-setting scuba dive to 452 feet in February 1990. To reduce his heart and respiration rate, Gilliam breathes through a snorkel at the surface without a mask for about 10 minutes. Still maskless, he breathes compressed air for an additional 10 minutes. His heart rate slows to an astounding 15 beats per minute and his respiration rate decreases from a normal 12 breaths per minute to 4 to 6 breaths per minute. Gilliam and others report these pre-dive maneuvers reduce air consumption, reduce narcosis and increase overall performance.

Chest compression also slows the heart. On land, test this yourself by taking the largest possible breath and holding it. Initially, your heart rate will climb rapidly—it might even double—but after 30 seconds it should descend and level off at a rate much slower than your normal resting rate. For example, if your resting rate is 70 beats per minute, it might climb to 120 in 10 seconds and then fall to 45 in the next 20 seconds. It will remain steady at the reduced rate until you release the pressure by exhalation.

When you take a deep breath and hold it, you're increasing the pressure in your chest. In response to the pressure, your vagus nerve (located in your chest and neck), causes a reflexive heart slowing. Emergency-room physicians use this phenomenon to a patient's advantage when they need to slow his heart. They might apply ice water to the patient's face and eyes, or they might have the patient take a deep breath and then tighten his abdominal and chest muscles. The result is often a dramatic slowing of the heart. Patients and untrained divers experience up to a 40-percent drop in heart rate. Trained divers can develop an even lower heart rate.

If you have an arrhythmia (a heart rhythm disturbance), you must seek medical advice before freediving. Even in healthy people, the diving reflex increases arrhythmias. In those with diseased hearts, especially after hyperventilation or diving in cold water, the diving reflex could initiate dangerous irregular heart beats.

Trained freedivers develop several other physiological adaptations that lead to deeper and longer dives. The spleen, acting as a blood reservoir, helps trained divers perform better. Apparently the spleen shrinks while diving, causing a release of extra blood cells. According to William E. Hurford, M.D., and coauthors writing in *The Journal of Applied Physiology*, the spleens of the Japanese *ama* divers they studied decreased in size by 20 percent when they dove. At the same time their hemoglobin concentration increased by 10 percent (volume 69, pages 932-936, 1990).

This adaptation, similar to one observed in marine mammals (the Weddell seal's blood cell concentration increases by up to 65 percent), could increase the diver's ability to collect oxygen at the surface. It could also increase oxygen delivery to critical tissues during the dive. Interestingly, the spleen's contraction and the resulting release of red blood cells is not immediate—it starts happening after 15 minutes of sustained diving. The spleen adaptation and other physiologic changes probably take a half-hour for full effect. This might explain why trained freedivers can dive deeper and longer after their first half-hour of diving.

There are other known adaptations: blood vessels in the skin and in the muscles contract under conditions of low oxygen (hypoxia), and blood vessels in the brain, heart and lungs dilate in order to provide more blood for these important organs. Changes in blood chemistry allow the body to carry and use oxygen more efficiently. These changes, in effect, squeeze the last molecule of available oxygen from nonessential organs. When the freediver surfaces and takes his first breath, the heart rate increases, helping to speed oxygen-enriched blood to the body. Most importantly, the diver's mind adapts to longer periods of apnea (no breathing). He can ignore, for longer periods of time, his internal voice that begins as a whisper but soon screams, BREATHE!

> **The diver's mind adapts to longer periods without a breath. He can delay the onset of the urge to breathe.**

THE GASES OF RESPIRATION: OXYGEN AND CARBON DIOXIDE

Oxygen is responsible for life but accounts for only about 20 percent of the air we breathe. The second you start breath holding, you consume oxygen and become progressively hypoxic. Hypoxia is the medical term for low oxygen in your blood. After a breath of fresh air, your body reverses hypoxia in just 5 seconds. The rate at which you use oxygen depends on your state of relaxation, your muscular activity and the depth you dive. Since these three factors vary with each dive, it's impossible to predict the safe duration of any particular dive. You've got to rely on your "internal computer" to tell you when it's time to surface.

While it's possible to reverse hypoxia in 5 seconds, muscular-oxygen debt takes minutes to correct. Your muscles are able to function in a low-oxygen environment by using alternate metabolic pathways that generate lactic acid. The use of these alternate metabolic pathways causes "oxygen debt" and the lactic acid produced causes a burning sensation in your muscles. You repay the debt during your surface interval between dives. Because these alternate metabolic pathways are less efficient than those you use in normal breathing, your oxygen debt is greater. Therefore, you must increase your time at the surface to repay this oxygen debt.

We've seen how oxygen is replenished at two rates through both gaseous and metabolic pathways. The same is true with the other important gas of respiration: carbon dioxide. If the dynamics of oxygen hint of unpredictability, the dynamics of carbon dioxide are absolutely confounding (for everyone except physiologists), especially in the face of exercise or hyperventilation. Carbon dioxide is the primary waste gas produced by metabolism. The movement of carbon dioxide in your body is slower than that of oxygen; it takes longer for carbon dioxide to reach equilibrium between your tissues, blood and lungs. Without proper rest and breath control, the two gases quickly become out-of-phase with each other.

Unlike oxygen stores, which always decrease during a dive, carbon dioxide levels may either rise after heavy exercise or fall after hyperventilation.

> *Without adequate rest between dives and the use of proper breath control, the balance between oxygen and carbon dioxide gases is upset.*

When your muscles exercise, they generate carbon dioxide. The average individual requires 3 to 5 minutes rest on the surface between dives to eliminate excess carbon dioxide; in some cases the interval is 10 minutes. When you make repetitive dives with inadequate surface intervals, or when you exercise vigorously, you risk accumulating excess carbon dioxide in your body—slow hypercapnea. You might notice a vague sensation of anxiety or unease and one or more of the following: a tendency toward slow but deep respiration, excessive salivation, nausea, a vise-like headache, exhaustion and cramps. Note how most of these symptoms resemble sea sickness. Getting out of the water long enough to eliminate the excessive carbon dioxide buildup resolves the problem; maintaining an adequate surface interval helps prevent it.

Another problem with the slow accumulation of carbon dioxide during freediving sessions is that it seems to progressively decrease the sensitivity of the breathing center. In other words, your mind stops reminding you to breathe. So you end up staying down longer than your body can really handle. High carbon dioxide levels contribute to diver blackout, as we'll explain next.

FREEDIVER BLACKOUT

You might think that shark attacks, line tangles and boat accidents are the freediver's worst fears; in reality those risks pale in comparison to the death and destruction wrought by diver blackout.

Blackout is the sudden loss of consciousness caused by oxygen starvation. Divers can experience two types of blackout. Shallow-water blackout occurs when divers ascending vertically in the water column undergo pressure changes. Static-apnea refers to blackout that doesn't involve a deep dive; it's generally related to breath-hold attempts in a shallow pool.

Shallow-water blackout strikes most commonly within 15 feet (five meters) of the surface, where expanding, oxygen-hungry lungs literally suck oxygen from the diver's blood. The blackout occurs quickly, insidiously and without warning. Beginning breath-hold divers, because of their lack of adaptation, are not generally subject to this condition. It is the intermediate diver who is most at risk. He is in an accelerated phase of training, and his physical and mental adaptations allow him to dive deeper and

> **Shallow-water blackout is the sudden loss of consciousness caused by oxygen starvation during the diver's ascent. Unconsciousness strikes most commonly within 15 feet (5 meters) of the surface.**

longer with each new diving day—sometimes too deep or too long. Advanced divers are not immune.

The beginning diver is very sensitive to carbon dioxide levels. These levels build even with a breath-hold of 15 seconds, causing your diaphragm to contract involuntarily and your lungs to feel "on fire." Normal divers reach their "breaking point"—the urge and need to breathe—well before their blood-oxygen levels become dangerously low. Remember, it's not the lack of oxygen, but the rise of carbon dioxide that signals your brain to breathe.

Hyperventilation is the potentially dangerous practice of increasing the rate and/or depth of your breathing in preparation for a dive. Many breath-hold divers reach depths of 80 to 100 feet and achieve bottom times of over 2 minutes by hyperventilating. The hyperventilating diver has "blown off" massive amounts of carbon dioxide, thus outsmarting the brain's breathing center. Normally metabolizing body tissues, producing carbon dioxide at a regular rate, do not replace enough carbon dioxide to stimulate this breathing center until the body is seriously short of oxygen. Trained divers can also short-circuit the desire to breathe by sheer willpower.

Hyperventilation causes some central nervous system changes as well. Practiced to excess, it causes decreased blood flow to the brain, dizziness and muscle cramping in the arms and legs. But moderate degrees of hyperventilation can cause a state of euphoria and well-being. This can lead to overconfidence and the dramatic consequence of a body performing too long without a breath: blackout.

PHOTO: TERRY MAAS

Brian Yoshikawa mimics a shallow-water blackout.

When Terry researched the subject of shallow-water blackout for *BlueWater Hunting and Freediving*, he was shocked to discover that most of the world's top spearfishers had experienced close calls with shallow-water blackout.

Damiano Zannini, M.D. reports that approximately 70 percent of the Italian divers who regularly compete in national and international spearfishing competitions have suffered one or more blackouts. It's interesting to note that *ama* divers, with their history of hundreds of years, experience a low rate of shallow-water blackout. They stick to a conservative dive profile—they limit the duration of their dives to one minute and rest between them. They also prefer to make many short dives instead of a few long ones.

The use of hyperventilation in preparation for freediving is controversial. No one disagrees that prolonged hyperventilation, after minutes of vigorous breathing accompanied by dizziness and tingling in the arms and legs, is dangerous. Some diving physicians believe that any hyperventilation can be deadly because of its unpredictable effects from person to person and from day to day. Other physicians, studying professional freedivers such as the *ama*, found that they routinely hyperventilated mildly and took a deep breath before descending. Their hyperventilation is very mild; they limit it by pursed-lip breathing before a dive.

> *Never attempt excessive hyperventilation—more than four rapid, deep breaths in preparation for a dive.*

All international scuba diver-training agencies including NAUI, PADI, YMCA and TDI consider hyperventilation unsafe if you take more than three breaths. The *U.S. Navy Diving Manual* (Volume 1, Air Diving) states, "Hyperventilation with air before a skindive is almost standard procedure and is reasonably safe if it is not carried too far. Hyperventilation with air should not be continued beyond three to four breaths, and the diver should start to surface as soon as he notices a definite urge to resume breathing."

Our advice: never attempt more than four rapid, deep breaths in preparation for a dive. This advice is frequently undervalued by unsafe divers. Simply put, hyperventilation is unpredictable. Instead of rapid hyperventilation, use deep, slow relaxation breathing similar to yoga breathing. Using a watch and a depth gauge, work out a comfortable dive profile and avoid exceeding its limits.

Pressure changes in the freediver's descent-ascent cycle conspire to rob him of oxygen as he nears the surface by a mechanism Terry calls the "vacuum effect." Gas levels, namely oxygen and carbon dioxide, are continuously balancing themselves in the body between the lungs and body tissues. The body draws oxygen from the lungs as it requires. The oxygen concentration (partial pressure) in the lungs of a descending diver increases as water pressure increases. As the oxygen molecules compact tighter in the compressed lung, they provide a temporary increase of oxygen available to the body. As the brain and tissues use oxygen, more oxygen is available from the lungs, provided the diver keeps descending. This process continues to work well as long as some oxygen remains in the lungs and the diver stays at his descended level.

The problem is in the ascent phase of the dive when the reexpanding lungs of the diver increase in volume as the water pressure decreases. The few oxygen molecules left in the lungs become widely dispersed. This results in a rapid decrease of available oxygen in the lungs to critical levels. The balance that forced oxygen into the body is now reversed. This vacuum effect (the reduced partial pressure of oxygen) is really a net flow of oxygen from the body to the lungs. In many cases carbon dioxide gas—the stimulus for breathing—may also decrease. These changes are most pronounced in the last 10 to 15 feet below the surface, where the greatest relative lung expansion occurs. This is where unconsciousness frequently happens. It is the result of a critically low level of oxygen, which in effect, switches off the brain.

While some divers experience warning signs of impending blackout—such as dizziness, light headedness, tunnel vision, seeing stars, sensation of heat or a sense of euphoria—most do not. Even if these signs do occur, they're often too little and too late. Frequently, the last thoughts of the blackout victim are, "I feel that I'm in trouble but the surface is just a few kicks away and I'm confident I'll make it…" The blackout is instantaneous and without warning.

During unconsciousness, a diver may continue to kick or swim because the muscles in his arms and legs can function for short periods with less oxygen than the brain. It is therefore important for dive buddies to note the attitude or angle of their friend's path as they come up from the depths. Unconscious divers may suddenly veer off to one side, arch their backs and spread their arms or sink back towards the bottom. Other victims reach the surface and bob up and down several times in their vertical plane (the "cork sign") without clearing their snorkel. Then they stop moving and float on their bellies without breathing.

The unconscious diver is now a potential drowning victim. If he floats, the vacuum effect will cease, and there might be enough residual oxygen to allow for consciousness to return. There is no guarantee that the shallow-water blackout victim will reawaken at the surface.

Researchers have identified a way to possibly explain why some divers do regain consciousness. The primary oxygen store in the body is obviously the lungs. However, at low concentrations, oxygen is also present in venous blood and bound to muscle myoglobin. When the ascending freediver reaches about 15 feet (5 meters), the lung-oxygen content becomes so rarified that the blood heading for the brain is drained of oxygen, and blackout follows. On the surface, the heart continues circulating oxygen-poor arterial blood through the tissues, where it mixes with blood slightly richer in oxygen and where it actually collects oxygen on the return trip to the lungs. In this scenario, the oxygen-depleted lungs now start to receive low levels of oxygen from these secondary oxygen stores found in the venous blood and muscles—just enough to reestablish consciousness.

In another scenario, the diver surfaces, takes a breath and then passes out. He regains consciousness after 5 seconds—the time it takes newly oxygenated blood to make the trip to his brain.

Sinking divers, on the other hand, do not benefit from this tenuous "second chance." While they have lost voluntary control, they still have other active protective reflexes. When a diver becomes unconscious, he stops holding his breath and air escapes. As water starts to enter the throat, the laryngospasm reflex causes the vocal cords to close, preventing water from entering the lungs. Rescuing a diver at this stage might require yanking his snorkel from his clenched jaw muscles, opening his airway and administering forceful mouth-to-mouth breathing pressure to overcome the spasmed vocal cords. Some recommend mouth-to-snorkel breathing as another way to get emergency oxygen into the distressed diver. An unconscious diver may be so deprived of oxygen that his face turns deep blue or black.

> *While some divers experience warning signs of impending blackout such as dizziness, light headedness, tunnel vision, seeing stars, sensation of heat or a sense of euphoria, most do not.*

> *It is important that divers resuscitated from blackout and near drowning seek immediate medical attention.*

"Dry drowning" is the term used to describe the condition when the laryngospasm reflex keeps water from entering the lungs. "Wet drowning" results from the early relaxation of the vocal cords and the subsequent entry of water into the lungs.

As oxygen starvation continues, death is so near that even the protective laryngospasm reflex relaxes, and within seconds, water enters the lungs. It is still possible to revive a diver at this stage, however, he will require hospitalization and intensive treatment. Water entering the lungs is very irritating to the delicate lining—fresh water more so than salt water. The irritation causes the lung tissue to swell and fill with fluid. Left untreated, this condition can become severe enough to prevent respiration and cause death by so-called "secondary drowning." This is why it is so important that divers resuscitated from blackout and near drowning seek immediate medical attention. Since this condition may take hours to develop, don't be fooled by the victim's apparent complete recovery.

After six to eight minutes without oxygen, the brain suffers permanent damage, although the heart often continues to beat after brain damage occurs. Cardiopulmonary resuscitation (CPR) at this point frequently revives victims to a vegetative state. CPR should always be administered to the drowning victim, no matter how much time he has spent underwater because the diving reflex and a cold environment offer the brain additional protection. Victims resuscitated in the field often experience an unusual recovery. They wake up screaming and then lapse back into unconsciousness, repeating this behavior over and over again.

Hyperbaric oxygen treatment, a new technique, offers limited hope to the comatose diver. Oxygen is administered in a decompression chamber identical to the one used to treat scuba divers with the bends. Theoretically, the oxygen, under pressure, penetrates the brain tissues and wakes up the damaged nerve cells.

Some think the oxygen reactivates nerve cells forced into involuntary hibernation by the prolonged lack of oxygen. This technique is controversial—not all neurologists believe it is effective—and it is expensive ($400 to $800 per hour). Patients undergo 60- to 90-minute treatments three to five times a week, sometimes for years. Many patients do not recover completely, suffering mental and physical deficits. For example, they might experience difficulty in speech and walking.

The following incident of shallow-water blackout is a chilling account of how this problem affects the best of divers. South African Jimmy Uys, a chemical engineer, has the distinction of holding the largest-fish record for any bluewater species—a 533-pound (242-kilogram) black marlin. Here is the story in his own words.

Date: May 1988

The place: The wreck of the "Produce" near Durban, South Africa, where four teammates and I were training for our National Spearfishing Championships. After diving for weeks on end, we felt extremely fit.

The incident: I went down to the bottom 100 feet (33 meters), just to the north of the main section of the wreck. Using the slight current, I slowly glided upward over the debris, when a 20-kilogram ignoblis (giant trevally) stopped in front of me. I shot it through its head and tried to fight it off the bottom. No luck! I released the line and just made it to the surface. My teammate Mark warned me not to take chances. His gun was also stuck on the wreck below.

Back on the boat, we planned our strategy. We would dive down together. Mark would pull the fish out of the wreck and kill it. I would cut the line from the spear and swim up with the fish.

We dove down together, hitting the wreck 20 feet (6 meters) down-current from the fish. Using valuable energy and oxygen we swam up-current to the fish. (Mistake No. 1)

It took a very long time for Mark to pull the fish out of the wreck and to stab it in the head. He left for the surface as I stayed behind. (Mistake No. 2) I cut the spearline and started to swim up with the fish on the spear, the nylon line wrapped around my hand. I was almost half-way up when the fish came back to life. This took me by surprise and the big fish pulled me back down about 20 feet (6 meters). Fighting with the fish, I suddenly realized that I had been down a very long time. I released the fish and headed toward the surface, using all the tricks in the book to save oxygen.

About 30 feet (10 meters) from the surface, I realized that I was not going to make it. My legs turned into jelly. A pleasing calm came over me and I felt relaxed. I thought "if this is the way to die, it is good."

The light faded from me and the last image mirrored in my mind was a soft orange sunset over the Langeberge on my dad's farm. I was gone...

An hour later: The heavy pounding of the speeding boat on the surface brought me round. I was lying on my back in the nose of the boat. When I opened my eyes, I saw a blurred vision of Mark behind the controls. I realized what had happened and said that I was all right just before I faded again.

My teammate's account: Mark saw me pass out but he was too tired to dive down to me. I sank back to the bottom.

Our boatman also realized that I did not surface and picked up all of the other divers. He took Mark and another teammate, Neil, and dropped them 20 meters up-current from my marker buoy.

Neil, who had never dived deeper than 60 feet (20 meters), made it to the bottom, looked around and saw a small piece of luminous green—my fin tips—sticking out of a hole in the wreck. He pulled me out of the hole and was met by Mark, who released our weight belts.

They pulled me onto the boat. Another teammate, Barry, the only one to have witnessed shallow-water blackout, said, "Forget it guys, Uys is a goner."

Sergeant Major Kloppers, an instructor in the "Rekkies," calmed everyone and declared that the group must try to save me. At that point, I had no heartbeat, I was not breathing and frothy blood streamed from my mouth.

Instead of rushing to the beach to get me to a hospital, the crew applied mouth-to-mouth resuscitation and heart massage on the boat. After 20 minutes, I suddenly stirred, coughed and started to breathe weakly.

The recovery: They stabilized me at the Scottsburgh hospital. They ambulanced me to Addington where I was dripped, strapped, oxygenated and injected for six days.

Static-apnea blackout

Static-apnea blackout results when a diver depletes all of the oxygen in his system. Unlike shallow-water blackout, there are no pressure changes—the diver simply runs out of air sitting or lying on the bottom. Unfortunately, alcohol is sometimes involved in static-apnea drowning.

Medical researchers feel that many pool deaths, classified as drownings, are really the result of static-apnea blackout. Most occur in male adolescents and young adults attempting competitive endurance breath-holding, frequently "on a dare." Drowning victims, especially children, have been resuscitated from long periods of immersion in cold water—30 minutes or more. The same is not true for victims blacking out in warm-water swimming pools. Warm water hastens death by allowing tissues, especially brain tissues, to continue metabolizing rapidly; without oxygen, irreversible cell damage occurs in minutes.

Static-Apnea Blackout

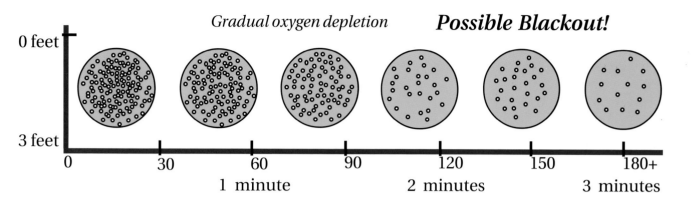

Gradual oxygen depletion

Possible Blackout!

0 feet

3 feet

0   30   60   90   120   150   180+

1 minute   2 minutes   3 minutes

Shallow-Water Blackout

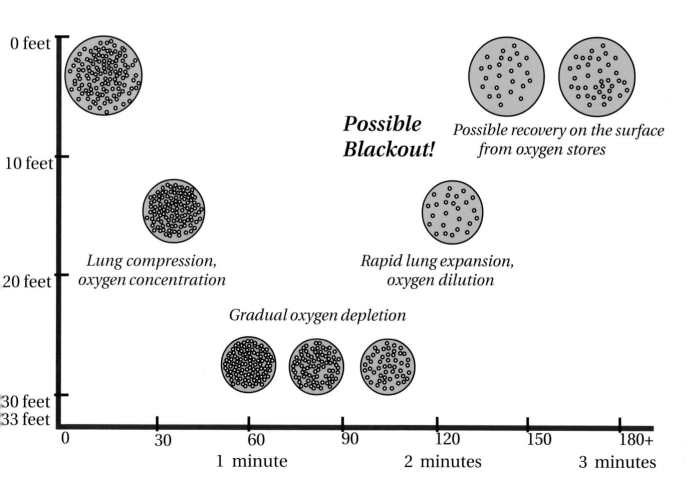

0 feet

10 feet

20 feet

30 feet
33 feet

Possible Blackout!

Possible recovery on the surface from oxygen stores

Lung compression, oxygen concentration

Rapid lung expansion, oxygen dilution

Gradual oxygen depletion

0   30   60   90   120   150   180+

1 minute   2 minutes   3 minutes

The key to rescuing those suffering blackout and near-drowning is immediate and aggressive resuscitation. If you're in the water, establish buoyancy for the victim and yourself. Yell for attention and immediately begin mouth-to-mouth or mouth-to-snorkel rescue breathing. Don't worry about swimming to the shore or to a boat. The quality of your resuscitation effort is far more important than the speed of transport. Remove the victim from the water as soon as is practical.

Once on the shore or in the boat, check for a pulse. If you don't find one, start the cardiac-resuscitation phase of CPR. Do not worry about water in the lungs. Do not perform abdominal thrusts in an effort to expel water as is typically shown on television. This procedure may force dangerous, acidic stomach contents into the lungs. Concentrate on rescue breathing. If oxygen is available, use it immediately, even if the victim regains consciousness. Seek immediate medical attention. Remember, don't be fooled by an apparent complete recovery. Lung damage may take hours to develop.

PREVENTION OF BLACKOUT

Shallow-water blackout was a hot research topic for diving physicians in the 1960s, when they worked out the basic physiology described above. They also studied the case histories of shallow-water blackout (SWB) victims, identifying several factors that can contribute to this condition. These include hyperventilation, exercise prior to and during the dive, a competitive personality, a focused mindset and youth.

Your breath-holding time ultimately depends on the oxygen contained in your last breath at the surface. Therefore, you need to limit the consumption of this most valuable commodity. Underwater, you should move effortlessly and efficiently. Every action must have a reason or you will waste precious oxygen. Remember that all body movements require oxygen and that the thigh muscles, one of the largest muscle groups, require more oxygen than most other muscles. Glide or pull yourself whenever possible. By keeping your external drag down and your swimming profile sleek, you will maximize the distance you can safely cover underwater.

Hyperventilation is dangerous because the effects are unpredictable in the same diver from day to day and from hour to hour.

Hyperventilation is dangerous because the effects are unpredictable in the same diver from day to day and hour to hour. The uncertain state of your oxygen debt and your carbon dioxide status is the reason for this unpredictability. Recall our discussion on oxygen dynamics and blackout: progressive hypoxia eventually causes blackout. Also, abnormal levels of carbon dioxide—high or low—hasten the onset of blackout.

One of the effects of low levels of carbon dioxide, caused by hyperventilation, is the narrowing of the blood vessels that supply your brain. The resulting reduction of blood flow to the brain causes you to lose consciousness more quickly.

As carbon dioxide levels rise slightly above normal, you experience an advantageous opening of your brain's blood vessels. You'll remain conscious longer at low oxygen levels. However, a higher concentration of carbon dioxide, as seen in slow hypercapnia, is dangerous because it hastens blackout. By itself, carbon dioxide in very high concentrations causes unconsciousness. High concentrations of carbon dioxide combined with low concentrations of oxygen is the classic definition of asphyxia.

After surfacing from a freedive, rest and continue slow and deep breathing to flush out carbon dioxide—this takes time.

How fast you ascend further complicates the carbon dioxide picture. A high rate of ascent, greater than 3 feet (1 meter) per second, lowers the carbon dioxide concentration in your blood. A slower ascent rate, less than a foot-and-a-half (a half-meter) per second, increases carbon dioxide. While it may not always be possible to moderate your ascent rate, it's interesting to know that even your ascent rate causes enough change in your carbon dioxide status to make its effect unpredictable.

After surfacing from a freedive, rest and continue slow and deep breathing to flush out carbon dioxide and help metabolize the accumulated lactic acid your muscles generate. This takes time. As a general rule, double the total time spent underwater to recover. For example, if you just completed a minute-and-a-half dive at 60 feet, then recover for 3 minutes before starting your next dive. For dives over 60 feet, your surface interval should increase to 5 to 10 minutes for each minute spent underwater. In shallow water, as your experience and fitness improve, you may shorten the surface interval.

Know the deadly effects of exercise underwater and plan to account for its effects. Freedivers learn to prolong their dives by profoundly relaxing their muscles (see the chapter on freediving technique). Most divers make minimal use of their muscles except when they fight a fish or free an anchor. Since exercise dramatically increases your use of oxygen, you need to end such dives early. As a physician writing in an Australian medical journal noted, "A common scenario for diving deaths in Australia is the experienced diver with weight belt on, speargun fired."

Researchers have found that the typical blackout victim is highly competitive and male (females appear to be more tolerant of low oxygen and high carbon dioxide levels than men). Many SWB victims are young—teens through early thirties. We don't know if this is because they lack experience or if some other unrecognized factor comes into play. The point is that young freedivers must be wary. Any diver who surfaces with the shakes, tunnel vision, starry vision or momentary memory loss has missed blackout by the narrowest of margins—just seconds. This should be considered a near-death experience and the dive should be examined for mistakes. There is more than one story about divers, rescued once from SWB, drowning on subsequent diving trips.

Focusing on a goal is dangerous. Many blackout incidents follow the diver's single-minded quest for game or for the freeing of an anchor. Try to leave 5 percent of your brain free to objectively monitor the progress of the dive. An internal warning should say, "I'm focusing too much. It's time to leave, drop my weight belt, drop my gun."

> *The typical blackout victim is highly competitive and male, and many are young—teens through early thirties.*

A good approach to shallow-water blackout is to weight yourself so that you will float at 15 feet. Your positive buoyancy makes it easier for others to assist you should you black out. Also, spontaneous recovery on the surface is not uncommon. Obviously, if you black out and sink, your chances of recovery are complicated and depend on help from an attentive and capable buddy diver. The last thing we want is a double or triple fatality caused by other freedivers over-extending their capabilities in an attempt to recover the primary victim. Whenever it's possible, carry a complete scuba unit for rescue or for anchor retrieval.

When spearfishing, use reels and drag lines to help tire the fish instead of fighting it underwater. Should your fish "hole up," buoy the spot and take your time extracting the fish from its cave. An unfortunate incident occurred in the 1985 United States National Freediving Championships, when defending national champion Phil Wisnewski drowned after attempting to free a large fish from a deep-water cave in a moderate current.

Dive and train with a buddy. Make sure he makes it to the surface and starts to breathe before you dive. When the visibility permits, alternate dives with your buddy. Keep a close eye on each other when it's deep. Deep is relative—it may be 30 feet (9 meters) for some and 80 feet (24 meters) for others. You know it's deep when you feel a little bit of apprehension or when the dive falls out of your usual dive profile. If you have to dive alone, use a line and a small buoy so others can monitor your activity and general location.

> *A good approach to shallow-water blackout is to weight yourself so that you'll float at 15 feet.*

Limit freedives to 90 seconds—longer dives tremendously increase the risk of blackout. Attempting breath-hold dives longer than two minutes requires a buddy/safety diver. You can make dives this long only by depressing your physiologic alarm or willfully ignoring the urge to breathe. At this point, almost everyone has a very low blood-oxygen level.

Is there some mechanical way to prevent blackout? Some suggest carrying a small bottle of compressed air, believing that a gulp of air might save them. Others have proposed a time-release buoy that will deploy after a certain interval underwater, thus floating the freediver. But reliance on compressed air makes you vulnerable to air embolisms and mechanical failure of the equipment. And a time-release buoy might malfunction in a cave or activate too soon or too late. Dependence on such devices is not recommended. But what if you could be accurately warned of impending blackout in time to act to prevent it?

Since blackout follows low blood-oxygen levels, a warning device monitoring blood oxygen would be ideal. Such devices exist today—they're called pulse oximeters and you'll find them in any setting where medical personnel administer general anesthesia. Through a small sensor, attached to the finger or the ear, the oximeter continually measures blood-oxygen levels. It's designed to warn anesthesiologists if the oxygen level in their patient's blood falls below a pre-set level they feel is safe.

Diving scientists have already used pulse oximeters to study Korean and Japanese freedivers. They placed the oximeters in pressure-proof back-packs and attached a sensor to the diver's ear. The investigators found that the oximeters functioned well underwater. An oximeter, equipped with an audible alarm, set to alert at a low, but safe level of blood oxygen might just save lives. This would make an excellent training tool. Maybe an enterprising company will consider manufacturing them.

SUMMARY

AVOID SHALLOW-WATER BLACKOUT

1. **Do not hyperventilate to excess—use no more than three or four slow, deep breaths.**

2. **Recognize that any strenuous exercise will limit your bottom time drastically; when you exercise, head for the surface much sooner than usual.**

3. **Recognize a dangerous situation when your mind starts to focus on a goal, and drop your weight belt.**

4. **Treat your weight belt as a disposable item; if in doubt, drop it. Bring a spare weight belt so that you're less hesitant to let it go.**

5. **Adjust your weight belt so that you will float at 15 feet (4.5 meters).**

6. **Don't attempt dives longer than 90 seconds.**

7. **If you must make a long or deep dive, make sure you have a buddy standing by on the surface.**

8. **Rest long enough between dives to flush out excess carbon dioxide.**

9. **Consider a swimming pool a dangerous place to practice endurance breath-holding. Always have an observer standing by to assist.**

10. **Learn the basics of CPR and think about adapting them to your diving arena, whether diving from shore, board or boat.**

Physiology—part II

In this chapter, we'll examine the effects of water pressure on your body and gear. The density and weight of water has profound effects on your body. Understanding the physiology of pressure and ways to cope with it are fundamental to successful freediving.

DIRECT EFFECTS OF WATER PRESSURE

Saltwater exerts a pressure of 14.7-pounds-per-square-inch (psi) for every 33 feet (10 meters) of saltwater. Every 33 feet is equivalent to the weight of our entire atmosphere, so we commonly refer to each 33 feet of saltwater as one atmosphere of pressure. For example, when you descend to a depth of 33 feet, you will have a total of two atmospheres (29.4 psi) compressing your body—one atmosphere of air and one of water. This total pressure is referred to as absolute pressure. Your depth-gauge reads only water pressure.

In physics, there is a gas law that explains pressure and volume relationships. Called "Boyle's Law," this concept is important to understand because it helps explain why you feel pain in your ears at the bottom of a swimming pool or why your wetsuit loses buoyancy in deep water. Boyle's Law states that the volume of any gas is inversely proportional to the absolute pressure. This means that as the external pressure increases on a volume of gas, it will compress that volume, by packing gas molecules closer together. Let's look at an example.

If your lungs had 6 liters of air in them at the surface and you then dove to 33 feet (10 meters), the volume of your lungs would be reduced by half of its surface volume (3 liters). This air did not escape; rather, the gas molecules compressed together causing the density of that air to double.

If you dived to 66 feet (20 meters), you'd have 3 atmospheres of pressure compressing your lungs to one-third of their original volume and the air inside would be three times denser.

Depth in feet (meters)	Pressure in Atmospheres	Absolute pressure (psi)
0	1	14.7
33 (10 meters)	2	29.4
66 (20 meters)	3	44.1
99 (30 meters)	4	58.8

As depth increases, lung volume decreases and the density of the air inside increases. Since the air inside your lungs is composed largely of nitrogen, oxygen and carbon dioxide, we can conclude that the concentration (partial pressure) of all of these gases will increase with depth. The density of gases is important because we need a certain partial pressure of carbon dioxide to stimulate breathing and a certain partial pressure of oxygen to keep us conscious.

> *Water pressure affects every gas space in your body and equipment—your ears, sinuses, lungs, stomach, wetsuit and mask.*

Boyle's Law affects every gas space associated with freediving, whether it's in your body or in your equipment. This includes the air spaces in your ears, sinuses, lungs, stomach, wetsuit and mask. At sea level, your body is under pressure from the weight of the air above. You don't feel this pressure because your internal pressures are "equalized" to the external air pressure. Since water is much denser than air, you'll feel its effects very quickly as you descend.

Squeezes

Because most of your body is made of non-compressible fluids, you'll feel the force of increasing pressure primarily in the air cavities of your head and chest. Generally, the first sign of increasing water pressure is pain in your ears. We call these pressure-induced changes in air cavities "squeezes." Divers must contend with ear, chest and mask squeezes. "Equalization" or "clearing" are terms used for the supplying of pressure from your lungs, throat and mouth to offset, or balance, external water pressure. Equalization pressure returns eardrums, sinus walls and masks to their former shape.

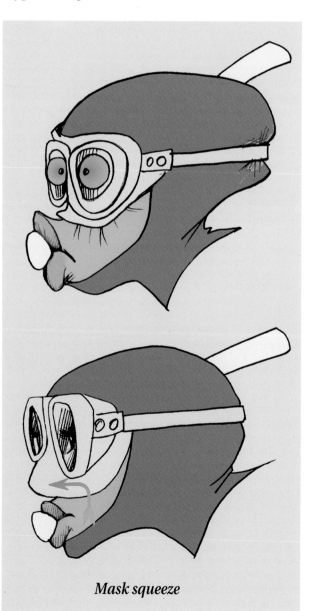

Mask squeeze

> *By breathing small amounts of air into your mask, you can offset the increasing pressure on your face plate. Because this air is precious, use just enough to release the squeeze.*

Mask squeeze

Unopposed water pressure on your mask causes pain, and coupled with a tight fitting mask strap, causes "ring around the face." Ignoring the discomfort and failing to equalize your mask will cause tiny blood vessels to rupture under the skin around your eyes and cheeks. Swelling and bruising may follow.

By breathing small amounts of air into your mask, you can offset the increasing pressure on your face plate. Because this air is precious, use just enough to release the squeeze. You may recover this air by inhaling during your ascent.

The best solution to mask squeeze is a low-volume mask. The less air in your mask, the less air you'll need to push it off your face. Some dive-mask manufacturers make volume-reducing inserts that take up any air space not used for vision. Similarly, you can modify the inside of your favorite mask by adding bits of rubber or silicone calk. Fill any air cavity not in your line of vision.

Middle-ear squeeze

Of the three kinds of ear squeeze—internal, external and middle-ear—it's the middle-ear squeeze that's most common. In fact, it's probably the single biggest cause of freediver dropout. As increasing water pressure forces your eardrums and sinus walls in, you feel pain. If you don't correct this squeeze early in the dive, you may suffer a ruptured eardrum—it's possible to injure yourself in water just 4 feet (1 meter) deep. Unlike scuba divers, who have minutes to equalize their ears and may need to equalize only several times a day, the freediver has just seconds to clear his ears and may need to clear them hundreds of times a day. Because of problems with ear anatomy and/or soft tissue responses to chronic allergy, some individuals will never be able to freedive.

An important segment of your ear-clearing anatomy is the eustachian tube. Its proper function is critical to successful ear clearing. For freediving, the ideal eustachian tube would be a wide-open, straight

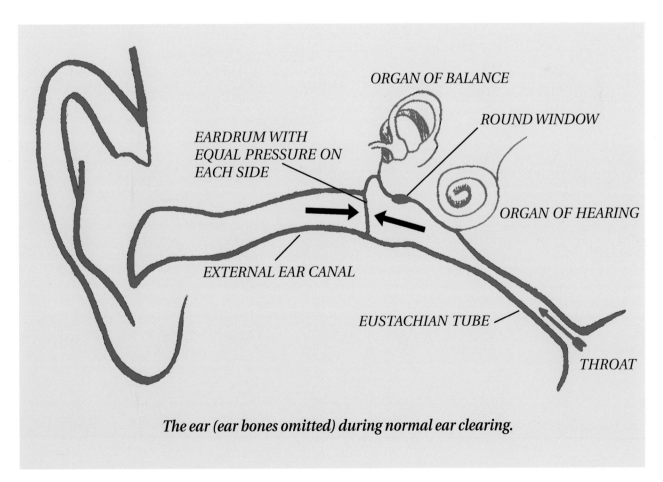

The ear (ear bones omitted) during normal ear clearing.

passage to the ear. Unfortunately, it's neither. Curving upward, this air duct is lined with the same mucous membrane that covers your throat—the very same mucous membrane that swells with allergies or colds. To equalize your ears, you seal your nose by pushing the bottom of the nose pocket against your nostrils (don't pinch) and gently blowing to force air through an open eustachian tube into your middle ear.

Swelling of the eustachian-tube lining blocks its opening, which makes ear clearing difficult, if not impossible. This explains why you should not dive with a cold, why persons with allergies have problems clearing and why some people with poor ear anatomy can't dive at all. Fortunately, for most people, there are methods available to manage middle-ear squeeze. We'll discuss the management of your eustachian tube and clearing methods in our chapter on diving techniques.

Signs and symptoms of a ruptured eardrum include nausea, pain, partial or complete hearing loss and loss of balance. Cold water rushing into your middle ear causes vertigo (total dizziness, nausea and confusion), which presents an obvious problem when you're underwater. If you have time, grab onto a solid object for stability and place your other hand over your injured ear to limit the entry of cold water. If you get disoriented and can't find the direction to the surface, which can happen in murky water, follow your bubbles. Get immediate medical attention. Expect your physician to prescribe antibiotics to prevent an infection. Normally, ruptured eardrums heal completely in 6 to 8 weeks without hearing loss.

David once suffered a ruptured eardrum playing underwater hockey. It was not inadequate equalization that caused his eardrum to burst, rather the sudden increase of external pressure to his ear caused by a fin slap to the side of his head. The water-hammer effect of the fin resulted in enough force to rupture the eardrum. After medical treatment, he resumed diving in 8 weeks. Check out the section on underwater hockey for details on headgear-protection equipment.

"Ear squeeze" and "block" are terms we use to describe the condition caused by a blocked eustachian tube, whether it's closed by soft tissue, mucous or both. Squeeze commonly occurs during descent. It is unusual on ascent because the shape of the ear and eustachian tube allow expanding air to escape readily. However, some divers experience dizziness or hear popping sounds when they ascend. This so-called "reverse block" occurs because a valve-like obstruction in the eustachian tube lets air into the middle ear but blocks its exit. This often happens after the use of decongestants

that wear off during the dive, letting the tissues swell and block off the eustachian tube.

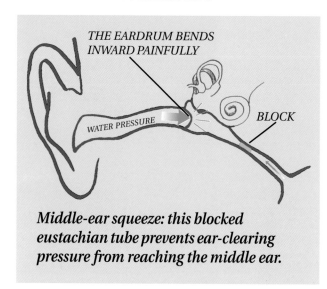

Middle-ear squeeze: this blocked eustachian tube prevents ear-clearing pressure from reaching the middle ear.

The problem with reverse block is that, as a breath-hold diver, you can't stop your return to the surface for air. If you experience reverse block, try to slow your rate of ascent if possible and stop diving until you're better. Uncleared reverse blocks are painful. After a long day diving in cold water, Terry developed a reverse block that took over an hour to clear. Chewing dinner must have helped to clear his eustachian tube because the loud series of squeals and pops he heard was followed by immediate pain relief and the return of his hearing.

Inner-ear squeeze

Your inner ear processes vibrations, transmitted through your eardrum, into sound. It also contains your organ of balance. Separating the air-filled middle ear from the fluid-filled inner ear is a thin membrane called the "round window." Rupture of your round window has serious consequences—deafness, debilitating dizziness, nausea and vertigo.

The round window can rupture inward or outward depending on the direction of force applied to it. It ruptures inward when you clear forcefully. Outward rupture occurs when you fail to clear your ears. In an attempt to equalize the pressure gradient between the middle ear and the inner ear, inner-ear fluid breaks the round window and leaks into the middle ear.

The symptoms of round-window rupture, usually noted immediately, may take up to 72 hours to develop. Suspect round-window rupture if you notice a background noise like ringing, hearing loss, intense vertigo and nausea. Seek medical advice because surgery, if recommended, is most successful when the repair is attempted early.

Veteran bluewater diver Bob Caruso says he'll never forget the debilitating effects of his round-window rupture. He'd been freediving for 4 to 5 hours at the Coronado Islands off San Diego. On the way back, in the boat, he felt fullness in his left ear, as if it wasn't clear. Blowing against his pinched nose, he made two quick, forceful attempts to clear the ear. "Suddenly, I felt as if I blew air straight through my head," he recalls.

It was 24 hours later when sudden vertigo brought him first to his knees and then onto his back. So intense was the nausea and dizziness that he could not even move his head. It took Bob three months to recover, but he never lost his hearing.

> *Obey the cardinal rules of ear clearing: equalize early, slowly and gently. Never try to clear your ears with short, quick bursts and avoid diving with a cold.*

ear. When he got off his boat, he felt like a drunk as he staggered to his car. Later that day, he developed severe vertigo that limited his locomotion to crawling from his car into his house. The next day, his vertigo improved. Most of the vertigo disappeared in the next month, but he remains deaf in the affected ear.

Neither diver had a cold or remembers difficulty in ear clearing. If you're deaf in one ear because of a round-window rupture, physicians recommend you quit diving to save your good ear. To help prevent round-window rupture, never clear your ears forcefully. Obey the cardinal rules of ear clearing: equalize early, slowly and gently. Never try to clear your ears with short, quick bursts, and avoid diving with a cold.

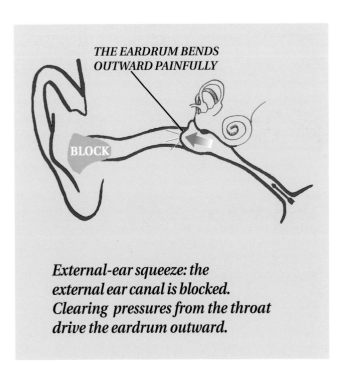

External-ear squeeze: the external ear canal is blocked. Clearing pressures from the throat drive the eardrum outward.

Inner-ear squeeze: either forced clearing or not enough clearing pressure may cause a rupture of the round window.

External-ear squeeze

Bill McIntyre was not so lucky. He'd made a tank dive to 90 feet and then freedove for an hour. On the way down, during his second tank dive, Bill cleared normally and suddenly heard a very loud ringing in one ear. On the surface, he realized he was deaf in that

External-ear squeeze occurs when something like an earplug, a tight-fitting wetsuit hood or excessive earwax blocks your external ear and prevents water from filling this area when you dive. A sealed, air-filled external ear canal develops a relatively low pressure as you descend. This causes the eardrum to bulge outward in attempt to equalize the air space. Typical symptoms include earache, fullness in the ears or ringing. It's common for divers to confuse this condition with middle-ear squeeze. Obviously, more clearing pressure is not the answer. Prevention is easy: make a small hole in your hood over your ear, or pull it aside when you make your first dive. Never wear earplugs.

As anyone who visits two California "fathers of freediving" Jack Prodonovich or Wally Potts soon learns, to tap their vast and undiminished knowledge, you've got to shout. Pointing to pictures of their early masks, with earplugs attached, they say, "See those earplugs. That's why we don't hear so well today."

Sinus squeeze

Sinuses are interconnected air-filled hollows encased within the bones of your face. They are lined by a thin layer of tissue containing small blood vessels. Similar to the lining of your throat, your sinus lining swells and makes mucous when you have a cold or allergies.

Since oral and nasal passages interconnect with your sinuses via small openings, they usually equalize without problems. If the sinus openings are blocked, you'll feel pain on descent. Blocked frontal sinuses (located above your nose and eyes) causes stabbing pain in your forehead. Blocked maxillary sinuses (located in your cheek above your teeth and beside your nose) cause pain in your teeth and below your eyes. The pain dissipates on ascent.

If you ignore the pain and continue to descend, blood vessels in your sinus linings rupture to equalize your sinus cavities. On ascent, expanding air in the sinuses expels the blood into your nose and mask. While blood in your mask is not a life-threatening sign, it's a good idea to stop diving for the day.

Thoracic squeeze

Thoracic, or chest, squeeze was once thought to be the major factor limiting how deep one could freedive. Physiologists once theorized that the lungs could not be compressed to a size smaller than one-quarter to one-third of their original volume.

If this theory is correct, how does Jacques Mayol dive so deep? At the surface, his expanded-lung volume is 7.22 liters, and at 90 feet (27 meters) it's 1.88 liters. Jacques continued his dive to an astounding 238 feet. According to Al Giddings in *Exploring the Deep*

Frontier, Mayol's body, at 240 feet, showed the effects of extreme pressure. His chest and abdomen appeared caved in with large skin folds around his chest. Later, Mayol became the first man to reach the 100-meter mark (328 feet).

How do Mayol, and others, like his successors Francisco "Pipin" Ferreras and Umberto Pelizarri, dive so deep? Like marine mammals, man experiences a large blood-volume shift into the thoracic cavity offsetting the loss of air. At 400 feet (122 meters) the lung's volume is reduced to the size of your fist! Pressure on the abdomen forces the diaphragm upward into the chest cavity. The liver and spleen release extra blood cells and reduce their volume in partial compensation for the pressure gradient found in the large venous blood vessels of the thorax. Relocation of blood and organs into the thorax allows divers to surpass the depth limits once predicted.

At what depth will the lungs collapse beyond recovery? Will major blood vessels rupture or the ribs crack? Will air in the ears and sinuses compress into the brain? Will the large vessels of the heart be kinked shut by the massive displacement of blood and organs into the chest cavity? Pipin believes he can reach 500 feet (152 meters). He and other ultra-deep divers will continue to push the envelope while at the same time redefining man's limits.

Decompression illness

It is possible for advanced freedivers to make enough closely-spaced, deep, breath-hold dives to accumulate an excess of dissolved nitrogen gas in their blood and tissues. This causes decompression illness, commonly known as the "bends." There is no requirement that you must breathe compressed air from a scuba tank to "get bent." Decompression illness (DCI) is a function of both depth and time, so the deepest freedivers are at risk—those capable of diving several hours at depths of 60 to 90 feet (18 to 27 meters). Most cases of DCI go unreported because the disease occurs most often in native, commercial freedivers.

When freedivers dive for long periods in deep water, they accumulate dissolved nitrogen in their tissues and in their blood. Because of the freediver's rapid ascent rate, the dissolved nitrogen actually bubbles out of the blood, fizzing like a freshly opened soda. These so-called "silent bubbles" are harmless unless the dissolved nitrogen content is so high that these bubbles become large enough to block blood vessels in the brain or exert pressure on vulnerable tissues. This is the bends.

You may have the bends after a long period of deep diving if you experience any of the following symptoms: bright flashes after ascent, vertigo, nausea, anxiety, weakness or numbness in a limb, painful joints, itching skin or difficulty with speech. For treatment, start breathing 100-percent oxygen and get to a recompression chamber as fast as you can.

Freediver DCI is not new. For years the pearl divers of the Tuamotu Archipelago suffered from the malady called "taravanna," meaning "to fall crazy." Signs and symptoms of taravanna include nausea, dizziness, partial or complete paralysis and mild joint pain.

World depth-record champion Pipin has been treated twice for decompression illness. Fifteen-time United States National Freediving Champion John Ernst felt the symptoms of DCI (pain in both shoulder joints) one evening after a day of deep freediving in cold water with an underwater scooter.

In Saint Croix during the late 1970s, Bret Gilliam treated a commercial lobster diver for numbness and joint pain following a day of deep freediving. After administering a field neurological exam, Gilliam was convinced that this diver suffered DCI, especially after he admitted to diving between 90 to 110 feet (27 to 33 meters) all day. While this diver declined hyperbaric treatment, he did respond to breathing pure oxygen for 30 minutes. After treatment, the lobster diver confided that this was not his first brush with DCI and that others had similar experiences.

Who should be concerned about DCI? Those who repeatedly dive deeper than 60 feet (18 meters) for longer than 2 minutes. Susceptible divers include competitive spearfishers diving to 120 feet (36 m) and more, commercial native freedivers and competitive deep-record divers. Divers who mix scuba diving and freediving in the same day should be especially wary.

Freedivers using underwater scooters should also be careful. Since the power of the scooter does most of the diver's propulsion for him, he's able to spend a significantly longer time at a greater depth. The scooter's fast ascent rate also contributes to the bends.

Although the odds of getting bent while freediving are small, especially if you monitor your time at depth and remain well hydrated, the real problem problems with DCI occur in those who freedive before, or after,

scuba diving. Surface intervals after compressed-gas dives are designed to be at sea level conditions and long enough to provide for the out-gassing of nitrogen. The danger is that freedivers can't accurately determine the levels of nitrogen dissolved in, or eliminated from, their bodies.

Scuba dive tables and computers do not provide a calculation for the freediving portion of diving. It has been erroneously suggested that scuba divers who plan to freedive after scuba should wear their dive computers. However, this violates the parameters used to design the computer making them inaccurate. Besides, you'd quickly become irritated with the sound of the ascent-alarm because of your repeated, rapid freediver ascents.

We recommend that you do not mix freediving and scuba diving. If you plan repetitive deep dives, calculate the entire duration of the dive at its deepest point, consult the decompression tables and stop diving well before decompression is required. Limit your use of scooters in deep water. Drink plenty of fluids to remain completely hydrated.

Air embolism

Air embolism is the condition that results when a ruptured lung leaks air into body tissues and blood vessels. It may cause heart problems and difficulty in breathing. While potentially dangerous, air embolism is rarely seen in freedivers. The usual cause of air embolism in scuba diving is the excessive lung pressures that develop when the scuba diver ascends rapidly without exhaling.

Generally, only freedivers who foolishly breathe from a friend's compressed-air source or breathe from an air pocket risk embolisms.

Without knowing it, Terry and his teammate John Ernst set themselves up for an air embolism. While scouting for a world championship in Spain, John discovered a cave 50 feet (15m) below the surface on the side of a vertical wall. Terry followed John into the cave where the pair discovered an air pocket. After removing their masks (not a bright idea), they talked excitedly about the beautiful sight of the glowing turquoise opening inside the dark cave. They speculated on the origin of the musty air they breathed.

When the novelty of the moss-ceilinged air pocket waned, the two took deep breaths and headed down to the cave entrance. On the way up, Terry was amazed

45

by the huge volume of air escaping from his relaxed throat. About half way to the surface, both divers realized that the extra bubbles were caused by the compressed air they breathed in the 50-foot-deep cave. They attributed their luck in escaping air embolism to their very relaxed state, which permitted the expanding air to exit easily.

Generally, only freedivers who foolishly breathe from a friend's compressed-air source or an air pocket risk embolisms. If you intend to breathe compressed air underwater, make sure you first become certified in scuba from a professional diving instructor. It could save your life. Remember, even if you blow bubbles out while ascending after breathing compressed air, your ascent rate may be too rapid to prevent air embolism.

> *Never dive with any drug until you have tested its effects on land several days before its intended use in the water.*

MENTAL AND PHYSICAL STRESS

Stress is a serious threat for the freediver: if it goes unnoticed or unchecked, it eventually leads to panic. Stress causes profound physiological changes. For instance, your body may release adrenaline, which stimulates your heart to beat faster and your blood vessels to constrict. Your breathing may become rapid and shallow while your oxygen consumption soars. If you don't eliminate the stressor, you're bound to panic and you may cause an accident.

A stressor can be any chemical, physical or mental factor that causes physical or mental tension. Mental stressors—such as fear, embarrassment, time constraints, excessive workload and anxiety—all lead to impaired behavior and perceptual narrowing (focusing on an unimportant item while ignoring something dangerous.) Physical stress includes equipment problems, sea sickness, fatigue, cold and injury.

Fatigue and exhaustion both contribute immensely to physical and mental stress. It's well known that the more tired you become, the more susceptible you are to sea sickness. Many freedivers insist on 8 to 10 hours of sleep before diving.

Some people become so debilitated by sea sickness that they make serious errors of judgment. We've seen divers become so sick that they ignored such dangers as a boat swim-step that could strike their head. While it's beyond the scope of this book to cover motion sickness, we'll offer a few hints for preventing this condition. The night before a dive avoid alcohol and rest well. On the day of the dive eat lightly several hours before boarding the boat and avoid heavy foods. On the boat, stay out of confined spaces, stay away from fumes and find the least-bouncy part of the boat—usually the center near the back. If you begin to feel sea sick, look at the horizon. Don't lean over to work on your gear; and consider eating soda crackers and drinking flat ginger ale.

Medications and wrist bands work well for many. Be sure to consult your physician before using any medication. The classic drugs for sea sickness are the antihistamines. Since their effects and side effects, including drowsiness, vary among individuals, you'll have to find the best for you. Be sure to take antihistamines in accordance with their instructions. Generally, you take them an hour or more before they're needed. Some divers take them a full day in advance.

For some, the scopolamine patch works well for sea sickness prevention. For others, the drug causes bizarre reactions and potentially dangerous disorientation. David once rescued two scuba divers on the surface before they began their dive. The scopolamine made them so confused they were not sure where they were, or what they were doing. This brings up a good point—never dive with any drug until you have tested its effects on land several days before its intended use in the water. The patch requires a prescription and needs to be taken with care. Besides visual problems (blurred vision) and mental disturbances (hallucinations), it causes a dry mouth. If patches are unavailable, some pharmacists can custom prepare them for you. Other remedies include homeopathic herbs—ginger root among others—and heavy-duty tranquilizers.

Fortunately, most physical stress is avoidable. Be familiar with your equipment. Never use new equipment in uncontrolled circumstances. Keep your gear simple. Make sure it's well maintained and fits properly. Remember, as Hercules said, "A man in armor is his armor's slave."

You can recognize the signs and symptoms of mental stress in yourself or your partner when you see a change in facial expression, a change in muscle tension, irregular movement, preoccupation with an item (i.e. depth gauge or speargun), a mood change, or rapid, shallow breathing. If you experience one of the above, simply stop, breathe, think and act. You've got to break the chain of events; if you don't, your panic may well cause an accident.

Practice your emergency skills regularly so that they become instinctive. Know your limitations and use common sense. When you attempt to increase your skill level, have a more experienced diver help you. Never push yourself beyond the point of comfort, and never attempt a dive beyond your ability for the sake of impressing others. Dive with a buddy; in freediving, there is safety in numbers.

> **When you start to shiver, get out of the water.**

Develop a sixth sense for diving—a total awareness of what is around you without having to turn your head to see. Examples include the freediver who senses a change in the current, or the deep diver who, after meditation and relaxation, knows he's going to reach his goal. The key to obtaining this sixth sense is constant diving and practice.

HYPOTHERMIA

Divers exposed to the cold develop hypothermia, a condition caused by the lowering of your body's central temperature—your core temperature. It occurs when heat loss exceeds heat production. Hypothermia can become life-threatening or so incapacitating that you're unable to overcome a dangerous situation. For instance, your decreased muscular coordination might prevent you from untangling yourself from a fishing line. Water conducts body heat 25 times faster than does air. Prolonged exposure to water, even tropical water, will suck off body heat faster than you can regenerate it.

Freedivers are especially vulnerable to hypothermia. In order to dive long and deep, they conserve energy by slowing their metabolism. Their muscles relax and their heart rate slows. Their economy of movement provides little heat-generating muscular exercise and they get cold.

Lowering your body temperature a few degrees Fahrenheit, from 98.6 to 93 (36 to 34 degrees Celsius), will cause your muscles to shiver and your heart to speed. Muscular power and dexterity suffer. Your hands and feet feel cold, but you remain alert.

When the body's core temperature drops another 3 degrees, from 93 to 90 degrees Fahrenheit (34 to 32 degrees Celsius), most people lose physical control, develop mental amnesia and actually lose the ability to shiver. Shivering is your natural defense mechanism against the cold. When you lose it, you're in trouble.

In severe hypothermia, the core temperature drops below 90 degrees Fahrenheit (32 degrees Celsius) and unconsciousness frequently develops. Victims may appear drunk, and clumsy and have slurred speech. Many drowning victims suffer hypothermia in addition to severe oxygen deprivation.

First aid for all types of hypothermia includes removing all wet items and placing the victim in a warm environment. Move the victim gently since rough movement can set off dangerous heart irregularities (arrhythmias). Apply mild heat, cover the victim with blankets and insulate him from the cold. If there are no blankets available, you can warm the victim with your own body heat by holding his body against yours.

For mild hypothermia, give the victim warm drinks but be sure to avoid alcohol or caffeine. Keep the victim warm for several hours or until he begins to sweat.

For moderate hypothermia, follow the steps above but keep fluids to a minimum. Give only small sips and then only if the victim is able to swallow without difficulty. Once you start the warming process, don't interrupt it. Fluctuating temperatures can cause serious problems in blood chemistry and heart function. Use warm circulating water like a Jacuzzi tub or use electric blankets. Concentrate your efforts on warming the victim's trunk. Warming his extremities may cause a drop in blood pressure or cardiac output because, when the blood vessels dilate, they send cold blood straight to the heart. Seek medical attention.

For severe hypothermia, seek immediate medical attention. Don't handle the victim roughly and don't give him any food or drink. Apply mild external heat to his trunk. Warm his body gently and slowly, don't interrupt the process and don't attempt rapid re-warming.

Hypothermia isn't necessarily a condition that occurs in a matter of hours. Sometimes hypothermia is progressive, occurring on multi-day trips. Your core temperature may cool without you realizing it. When you return to the warm surface water after a

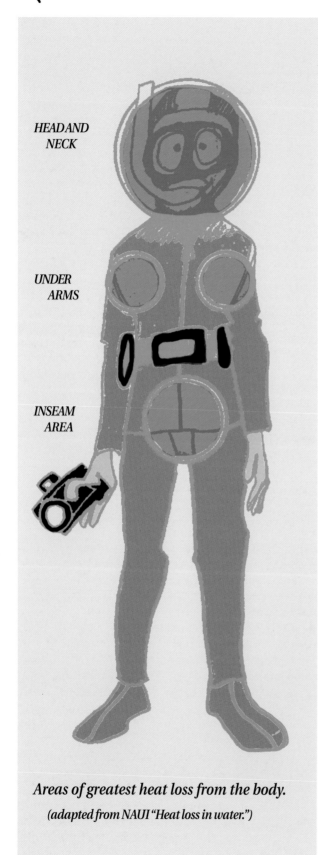

HEAD AND
NECK

UNDER
ARMS

INSEAM
AREA

Areas of greatest heat loss from the body.

(adapted from NAUI "Heat loss in water.")

dive into a thermocline, you will experience superficial skin re-warming that masks your slow heat loss. Each successive day increases your "thermal debt." Progressive hypothermia does not cause shivering, but you will experience fatigue and

> *Progressive hypothermia often occurs on multi-day trips. It's common to experience a gradual cooling of your core temperature without being aware of it.*

loss of enthusiasm. You may have hypothermia if you're too tired to care for your equipment or you become excessively sleepy after diving.

Once again, prevention is the best advice. Make sure that your wet suit or dive skin is suitable for the environment. Repair any holes or rips. Dive only when you're rested, nourished and hydrated. As a way of warming up, urinating in your wetsuit is analogous to drinking alcohol: both make you feel warm, but they actually cause your skin blood vessels to open up and radiate away your body heat. Once you start shivering leave the water.

HYPERTHERMIA

It might seem odd that freedivers should consider the possibility of hyperthermia—excessive core temperature, but it's a very real problem when you wear wetsuits in the sun. While rare, it is possible to develop one of the two forms of hyperthermia: heat exhaustion or heat stroke.

Heat exhaustion results when you develop a body-salt imbalance due to excessive sweating. You may feel hot or fatigued, and your skin may feel cool and clammy. To treat heat exhaustion, take off your wetsuit, find shade, rest and drink cool fluids. Never consume ice-cold drinks because rapid core cooling radically changes your blood chemistry and could cause dangerous heart arrhythmias. Drink fluids containing salts and sugars—sports drinks such as Gatorade or Powerade work well.

Heat stroke is the most serious form of hyperthermia since it involves a rise in body temperature due to dehydration and the loss of the ability to sweat. Sweating is your first defense against hyperthermia, and losing this ability is serious. Signs and symptoms include those found in heat exhaustion except that the skin is hot and flushed. Immediately, but gradually, cool the entire body using the same techniques for heat exhaustion, and seek medical attention.

> *It might seem odd that freedivers should consider the possibility of hyperthermia, but it's a very real problem with wetsuits in the sun.*

Preventing heat stroke is quite simple. Avoid prolonged exposure to direct sunlight while wearing your wetsuit. Keep wetsuit accessories off until just before you enter the water. If you wear a wetsuit in the sun, take an occasional swim in the water. Drink plenty of fluids throughout the day.

Heartburn

Heartburn, or pain in your esophagus, can be a problem for freedivers, especially those prone to this condition. Normally, a valve at the top of the stomach confines the acids of digestion below the esophagus. When these acids leak upward, out of the stomach, they burn the esophagus.

Freediving aggravates this condition for several reasons. Simple immersion increases pressure on the stomach by about four times and distorts the stomach-esophagus valve so that it leaks more easily. The unfavorable effects of gravity when you're floating or diving downward makes matters worse. Novices, using improper ear-clearing techniques, may swallow air, which also interferes with the stomach-esophagus valve.

You can prevent heartburn by eating non-acidic foods before you dive. Avoid fruit juices and carbonated drinks, and learn how to clear your ears without swallowing air.

For those of you who have problems with heartburn, consult your physician. Your doctor might recommend acid-neutralizing antacids such as Tums, or he may recommend a drug that blocks stomach-acid production, such as Tagamet or Zantac.

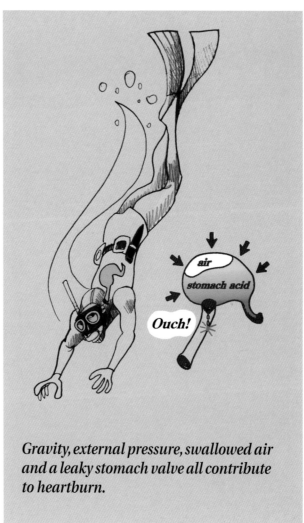

Gravity, external pressure, swallowed air and a leaky stomach valve all contribute to heartburn.

Nutrition and Dehydration

Even relaxed freediving requires an astounding amount of energy, much of which your body uses to produce heat. Freediving burns more calories per minute than any activity other than fast axe-chopping, according to scientists at the University of California at Berkeley. They estimate the average 175-pound diver burns 20 calories per minute, or a whopping 1,200 calories per hour. And since some freedivers often spend six to eight hours per day in the water, this means only one thing: they've got to eat.

We recommend loading up on carbohydrates the night before you dive—up to 2,000 calories of such foods as pastas, breads, starchy vegetables and fruits. In the morning, eating a light-carbohydrate breakfast will sustain you for up to three hours. After that, you must re-nourish yourself. We experimented with all sorts of liquid formulas, such as honey dissolved

49

in orange juice. Unfortunately, while these liquids did supply us with energy, they also burned our throats when we inverted for a dive.

There are diet supplements that provide energy and do not cause heartburn. Ensure and Sustagen, both available in drugstores, are medically complete liquid diet preparations designed for patients who cannot chew. Nutrament and Boost are body-building food-supplements packaged as high-caloric liquids. Both kinds of drinks work very well. These foods taste better when you drink them cold, and their water content helps prevent dehydration.

Dehydration contributes to fatigue, headache, a general decrease in athletic performance and the possibility of bends after repetitive deep dives. Divers dehydrate for two reasons: first, breathing through a snorkel uses dry air. Air breathed through a snorkel bypasses the sinuses and nasal cavities—humidifiers that normally add moisture to inhaled air. Bypassing these water traps allows extra water to escape the body.

> *Even relaxed freediving requires an astounding amount of energy. This means only one thing: you've got to eat.*

The second cause of water loss is a condition called "immersion diuresis." Immersing your body in water stimulates the kidneys to increase urine output.

You must compensate for your water loss by drinking extra water. It's easy to become so enthralled with your underwater experience that you either forget to take water, or simply don't want to interrupt your dive for a trip back to the shore. Consider carrying a water bottle on your float. Besides rehydrating you, the fresh water makes a great mouth rinse after salt water diving.

While you need not become an athlete to enjoy freediving, the sport does encourage a healthy life style. The intoxicating mental absorption you experience in a day's freediving replaces your day-to-day worries and refreshes your psyche for the week. Armed with the knowledge of your physical and mental adaptations and limitations, you should enjoy many breathless, underwater adventures with comfort, confidence and ease.

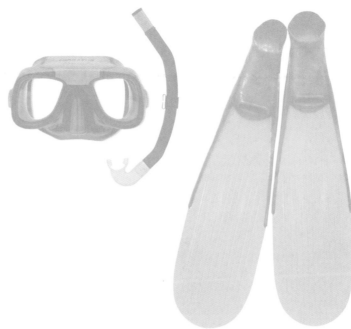

Freediving gear

Freediving gear is your passport to the marvelous universe underwater. Facemasks clear your blurred vision to expose an enchanting world more vast than any pool and more colorful than any aquarium. Fins transform your legs into dolphin-like appendages, wetsuits give you a whale-like skin that feels warm and safe and weight belts help you achieve true weightlessness. Fully equipped, you're almost a fish!

As simple as freediving gear is, you still have many choices. In some instances, you can even build your own equipment. When evaluating freediving gear, your primary concerns should always be safety, comfort and fit. What will keep my fins from falling off? How much weight must I use? The following should help prepare you to answer these and many more important questions about your gear.

MASKS

A facemask provides clear vision underwater. The mask best suited for the freediver is small and comfortable and contains a low internal-air volume. The faceplate lens is made of safety or tempered glass to prevent glass shattering into the eyes. A nose-pocket is necessary for mask clearing and should be large enough for you to seal your nose for ear equalization.

The water-glass-air interface, common to all masks, causes two problems: magnification and "mask squeeze." Light rays, traveling from an underwater image to your eyes, bend, or refract, as they pass through the lens and the air behind it. The final image appears 25 percent larger and closer than it actually is—an important consideration when you've got to estimate the size of your catch to comply with fish-and-game laws.

Mask squeeze results from the force applied to the mask from the surrounding water pressure. Unopposed, this force will eventually compress the air under the faceplate and crush the mask painfully to your face as you descend. To counter this external pressure, you must supply air from your lung reserves by blowing through your nose into the mask. This equalizes the pressure on each side of the lens and relieves the "squeeze." Refer to *Physiology—part II* for more information on this subject.

Equalizing pressure in the mask requires a significant amount of air—the freediver's most valuable commodity. The smaller the volume of air in the mask, the less air you lose. Consequently, you need a low-volume mask. Should you flood your mask accidentally, you'll find its low volume easier to clear. Some manufacturers offer volume-reducing inserts. You can make your own with bits of neoprene foam and silicone caulking. Fill all the space not used for vision.

Besides air volume, there are three other important considerations in your selection of a mask: fit, peripheral vision and nose pocket. Test the fit of the mask by brushing the hair from your face and placing the mask on without using the head strap. Inhale gently through your nose. The suction should

Of the many masks available, we suggest a low-volume model with two lenses and a dark skirt, like the top and bottom styles.

Removable magnifying lenses are an asset for those who use bifocals.

be strong enough to hold the mask to your face as you shake it side to side.

Test peripheral vision by holding your finger out to the side. Stand in the same place each time you compare your visual field with something on a nearby wall. As for the nose pocket, make sure it feels comfortable. For successful ear clearing, you should be able to easily seal your nose by pushing up against the bottom of the nose pocket with your thumb and first finger. If you dive with gloves, bring them with you to judge how well they perform.

Don't buy a plastic lens: it scratches and yellows. Avoid windows at the sides of the mask. We prefer masks with black skirts because we believe they help focus your vision toward the front. The black sides prevent movement off to the side from distracting you. They also prohibit strong peripheral light from confusing your retina.

Marine biologist and yellowtail world-record holder Mark Steele has another view. "After trying both styles—clear or black skirt—I use clear because it helps me detect fish from the side," he says. "More times than I can count, I have been alerted to fish off to my side by noticing movement through the clear skirt. This gives me an instant more to get into position with my camera or spear."

Mask skirts are made from rubber and, more expensive but more durable, silicone. Besides being hypoallergenic, silicone is clear or translucent, which is a benefit for those feeling claustrophobic behind a black rubber mask. "Silicone lasts longer," says New Zealand freediver Judy Johnston. "The only problem with silicone I've heard is when a rat ate my friend's mask—and his shoes, too."

You can correct your underwater vision with either contact lenses or ground-glass lenses. Physicians generally prefer the use of soft lenses over hard lenses. Get your doctor's advice. Be aware that water flooding a mask will sometimes dislodge, or even wash out, a contact lens. If this occurs, you may be able to find the lens near or in the nose pocket.

If you prefer a mask with corrective lenses, there are two types to choose from: custom or store-bought inserts. The best are custom lenses ground to your prescription and bonded to the inside of the faceplate. They correct for complicated visual problems such as astigmatism. An additional one-half-inch (12 millimeter), half-circle magnification lens, bonded near the bottom of one corrective lens, makes a serviceable bifocal. While quicker to install and less expensive, the store-bought lenses are less exact and cannot account for astigmatism.

FINS

Fins, along with the mask and snorkel, are the most essential freediving gear. In the late 1930s, the first North American freedivers explored the waters off La Jolla, California, with only their homemade facemasks. Several years later they discovered fins. Jack Prodonovich still expresses awe over his first swim with fins. "It was amazing," he recalls. " I couldn't believe my hair flowing backward in my wake. The whole unexplored kelp forest below 20 feet (6 meters) was now opened for us!"

Fins increase the freediver's efficiency and mobility. Freedivers agree that their fins should be about 39 inches (90 to 110 centimeters) long. A fin's blade produces a wave of displaced water that propels you forward. The larger the blade, the larger the wave. Only the water that is deflected straight behind the fin, along its long axis, provides push; water spilling over the sides represents wasted energy. Various manufactures use ribs and water-deflection devices to maximize the efficiency of their fins.

Your choice depends on what kind of diving you'll be doing. Soft, flexible fins are the best for all-around freediving. Their flexible fin blades produce, after the initial thrust, a gentle recoil, making them both more efficient and less fatiguing than stiffer blades. Very stiff fins are reserved for deep-diving attempts. Stiff-blade fins produce greater power but also require more energy to operate. Surface divers who use them tire quickly and experience cramping in their calves and foot arches. Moreover, very stiff fins can aggravate an existing lower-back problem.

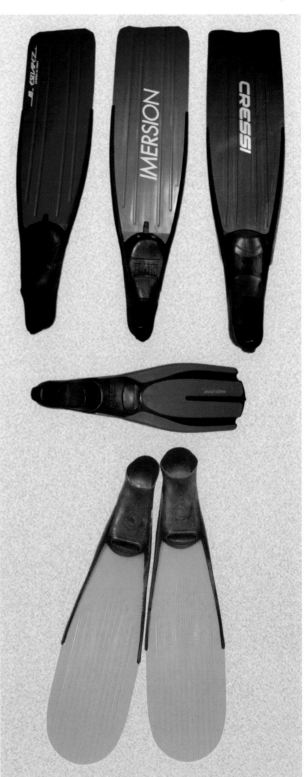

There are a large number of long-bladed freediver fins—all excellent, all European.

Deep-endurance divers, who dive vertically, prefer stiff fins because they can apply enough power to the stiff blades to begin their vertical descent through the water column early. After a few surface kicks, they pass the point of neutral buoyancy, where they cease to kick and glide down. On the return toward the surface, stiff fins also help overcome the twin anchoring effects of the weight belt and a partially collapsed wetsuit. Deep divers use large initial fin strokes to start their ascent; then they use smaller, streamlined kicks to continue upward.

Monofins, constructed with a single blade and two foot pockets are standard for competitive fin-swimmers. We'll discuss their design in the chapter on fin swimming. Interestingly, a considerable number of European spearfishers hunt pelagic (open water) fish with these fins, dolphin-kicking their way through the open water. In Hawaii, dolphin lovers use these fins to keep up with the speedy dolphins and interact with them almost as equals.

Fins should fit snugly and feel like a natural extension of your leg. Your first set of fins should be very flexible. Experiment with stiffer fins as your technique improves and leg muscles get stronger. One French company makes a versatile fin, offering five fin blades of varying stiffness. Other fin manufactures make models with interchangeable blades.

Foot pockets come in two types, open and closed. Open pockets use the traditional strap behind the heel to hold your foot in the fin pocket. An adjustable strap makes it easy to change the size of the foot pocket to accept the different sized booties required in water of different temperature. One problem with this design is that if the strap slips a little with each swim stroke, you'll waste energy. Also, the open-pocket produces drag and the large strap can snag kelp or monofilament fishing line. Finally, because straps and buckles break, you'll need to inspect them before each dive.

The closed, or full-foot-pocket fin is a better design for most freediving. It's streamlined and transmits more energy from your legs to the fin blade. Freediver Nuno Battaglia makes the case for this design when he says, "Picture running a marathon in a pair of sandals instead of running shoes."

One problem with full-foot pocket fins is that they can be dislodged from the foot when the fit is poor or in heavy surf or deep water. A wave of water can catch the heel of the foot pocket and pull the fin off your foot. When diving deep in cold water, the thick boots required can compress enough to make the fin become quite loose. David once lost a fin in deep water. "I was diving deep with a thick wetsuit and lots of lead," he recalls. "Because I had to kick so hard to get off the bottom, I was worried about losing a fin. I did precisely that at the bottom of a 60-foot (18-meter) dive. After dropping my weight belt and speargun, I put my legs together and used a modified, one-fin dolphin kick to reach the surface."

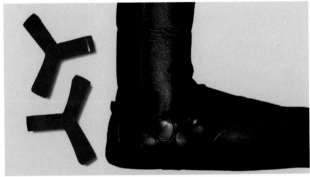

Fin keepers prevent your foot from being pulled out of a full-pocket fin.

Fin keepers, also known as "fixie-poms" or "poms," help prevent your foot from being pulled out of the full-pocket fin. Three interconnected rubber straps wrap the foot pocket to your heel, making an accessory foot strap. While most freedivers find them unnecessary, poms are useful when your fins do not fit well, when you need one-hundred-percent security or when you enter heavy surf.

A full-pocket fin, like the lower model, is best for freediving.

Because of the excitement of the dive and the numbing effects of cold water, you might not notice that your fins are causing deep skin erosions on your feet or ankles. Sometimes these painful lesions take weeks to heal. To protect your feet, you'll need to wear boots or socks. Use athletic socks in warm water and neoprene booties in cold water.

Snorkels with two valves are easier to use, especially by beginners. Despite the added bulk and increased maintenance requirements, some expert freedivers also prefer them. The purge valve, located at the bottom of the J, jettisons accumulated water out of the bottom when you blow. A small rubber diaphragm makes this valve open only one way,

Bill Ernst suggests using an extra half-boot to help retain your fins.

National Champion Bill Ernst designed a clever half-boot to help him retain his fins securely. First, he pulls the toeless boot on his foot and then over his heel. After he puts the full-foot pocket fin on, he covers the fin's heel by pulling the second boot back over the heel. The second boot offers both security and warmth.

When shopping for fins, bring along a pair of booties to assess the fin's fit. The correct stiffness is difficult to judge. Ask the salesperson to let you try a pair for a couple of hours for a test-run in the water. If your choice narrows to two models, choose the one with the most flexible blade.

SNORKELS

The snorkel, a "J"-shaped tube that conducts air to your mouth when you're face down in the water, conserves your energy because you needn't raise your head for a breath. A snorkel also lets you enjoy an uninterrupted view of the activities below.

Your best snorkel choice is a simple design—a hollow tube connected to the mouthpiece. Because there are no valves to break, a simple snorkel is good for remote locations. With practice, you'll become adept at sensing water entering the tube. When this happens, quickly stop inhaling and blow out with a short burst of air. This clears the snorkel and only rarely will water enter your mouth.

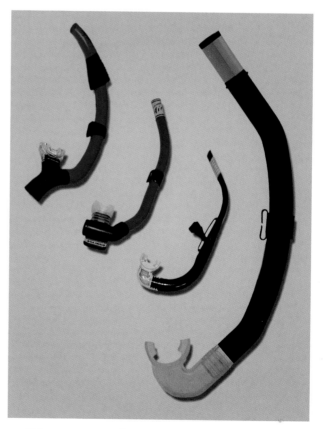

We recommend you choose a snorkel with a simple design like the bottom model.

preventing water intrusion. Another valve, located near the top of the snorkel, is supposed to divert splashed water from entering the tube.

The most important consideration is mouthpiece fit and comfort. Check for irritations. Does the flange place pressure on your gums? A few hours of swimming and diving with an ill-fitting flange can ulcerate the gums and possibly cause them to permanently recede from the necks of your teeth. Soft mouthpieces are generally the most comfortable, but be aware that extra-soft mouthpieces flex and distort during fast swimming.

The mouthpiece should hold your teeth a comfortable distance apart. If your jaws are too close, your air passage will be restricted; if they are too wide, your jaw joints can develop painful muscle spasms. One way to ensure that your mouthpiece fits comfortably is to use a snorkel equipped with thermoplastic teeth inserts. You heat the inserts in boiling water, let them cool just enough so you can tolerate the heat, and then bite into the softened material. The result is a perfect registration of your bite. You control both the position of the flanges against the gums and the amount of distance between your jaws.

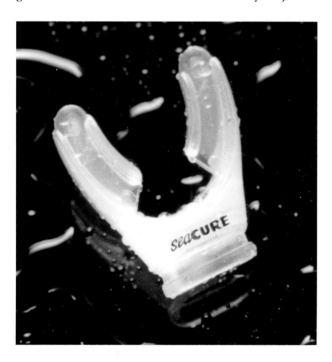

An example of a custom-moldable mouthpiece.

The snorkel's bore diameter is another important consideration. The volume of air contained in the snorkel adds to the "dead space" of your breathing apparatus. Dead-space air is the column of air between the end of the snorkel and your lungs that remains un-refreshed by a breath. Too much dead-space air impairs your breathing efficiency.

Small-bore snorkels have two advantages: dead-space air is reduced, and there is less water to expel when you surface. These snorkels are best suited for smaller individuals such as women and children. Larger people require a wider bore because the increased internal diameter causes less resistance to air flow, which makes breathing easy. However, as the bore diameter increases, so does both dead space and the amount of water you must clear at the surface. A modification of the basic design, the chambered snorkel, uses several full-length parallel chambers for easy clearing and breathing.

Some European divers prefer long, thin snorkels. They believe this design forces them to take long, slow, deep breaths, which promote relaxation. They say their tranquility is disrupted when they take the quick, deep breaths possible with larger bore snorkels. We do not prefer the long, thin snorkels because they increase your resistance to breathing as well as dead space.

Two-holed rubber or silicone snorkel keepers attach your snorkel to the mask strap. Sometimes even a correctly fitting mouthpiece can irritate your mouth if the snorkel's attachment is incorrect. When you start your dive, make sure the attachment lets the snorkel lay passively in your mouth without push or pull. Snorkel keepers sometimes squeak or allow the snorkel to flap excessively in the water. If this happens, try a different keeper or use two together.

In general, use the shortest snorkel for the prevailing water conditions. A shorter model works best in calm water and in underwater hockey games. It also performs better than a longer one against a current because there is less drag and less material to slap the side of your head. David carries two snorkels, one of standard length, and one that is four to five inches (11 centimeters) shorter—just long enough to clear the surface.

Several European manufacturers make an "anatomic" snorkel. It's designed to follow the contours of the face closely. By eliminating the deep J-bend, where the tube aims toward the surface, this shape decreases both dead-space air and water resistance.

For those of you who like to make your own gear, it is possible to design or customize your snorkel. You might even make it curve up and over to the middle of the top of your head for a form-fitting low profile. Find a plastic or acrylic tube with the desired bore. Using a hot-air gun, heat the tube in sections and form each section according to your design. The tricky part in this process is to prevent the tube from kinking and

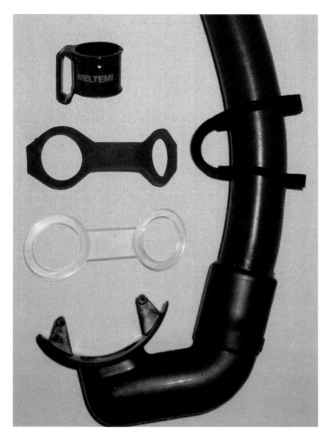

Snorkel keepers.

collapsing the bore at the bend site. Find an old-fashioned window shade mechanism and remove the spring. Use this spring, or alternatively fill the barrel with shot or sand, to maintain the bore's circular shape at the places you bend it.

No matter which snorkel you choose, comfort is the key. Make sure the mouthpiece fits well and that the barrel has adequate bore width and length.

WETSUITS

Wetsuits insulate you from the cold and protect your skin from reef abrasions, sea urchin spines and such poisonous creatures as fire coral and jellyfish. The "wet" in the word "wetsuit" refers to a thin layer of water that leaks into the small spaces between your skin and the suit.

Neoprene rubber became the standard material for wetsuits in the late 1950s. It makes a stretchable, form-fitting second skin. Tiny sealed bubbles of

nitrogen in the material form the actual insulation. Because these bubbles compress under pressure, the size and effectiveness of your wetsuit decreases with depth. After a season of many deep dives, the insulating bubbles break down and join, causing the material to become spongy and less effective.

The wetsuit's ability to insulate you is determined by its fit and its thickness. The best wetsuits, described by their manufacturers as "semi-dry," fit so closely that little, if any, water enters beneath them. Water circulating through your wetsuit because of leaky seams or poor fit will quickly chill you.

Your wetsuit should fit as snugly as possible without excessively restricting your body motion, respiration or blood circulation. A collar that is too tight, compressing the great blood vessels of the neck, can cause feelings of claustrophobia and panic. While zippers are convenient for getting the suit on and off, they are stiff and leaky—two efficiency robbers. Zipperless, pull-over tops are best. If you need zippers, keep them small.

Critical areas to check for a snug fit are the armpits, groin and the small of the back—all areas that collect water. You can fill the potential void in your back by gluing a 3-inch (8 centimeter) strip of neoprene inside the wetsuit over the lower back. Good tailoring takes care of the other water-collecting spaces. Special seals, called "skin-in-seals" in the United States and "Aqua Stop" in Europe, help make the suit semi-dry. They are made from one-sided neoprene strips fashioned into gaskets at the suit's wrists, ankles and neck.

The casual freediver might consider an off-the-shelf model, but the serious diver who intends to spend many hours in the water needs a custom-made suit. The warmest suit design employs a zipperless, full-sleeve top, extended to cover the hips, with a crotch strap connection in the groin and a hood attached at the head. "Farmer John" pants extend from the ankles well past the groin, over the trunk, to just below the neck, where they end in two shoulder straps. Since more than 20 percent of your body heat can be lost through your scalp, your hood must fit well. This design is so effective that when David wears such a suit only 1/8 inch (3 millimeters) thick, he feels he's as warm as an individual wearing a 1/4-inch (6-millimeter), off-the-shelf suit.

The advantages of a thin suit are several: they're comfortable and there is less buoyancy change at depth, therefore, the suit requires less weight. Wearing his 1/8-inch suit, David uses 8 pounds (3.6 kilograms) instead of 16 pounds (7 kilograms) and it's more streamlined.

There is a large variety of wetsuits available to meet your needs.

Wetsuit material varies in thickness. In the American system, sizes range from 1/8, 3/16 and 1/4 inches; in the metric system, corresponding sizes are 3, 5, 6.5 and 7 millimeters. The 1/4-inch (6.5- or 7-millimeter) suit is considered standard for cold-water diving conditions such as those you'll find in New England, Northern California and New Zealand. In warmer water, you'll use a thinner material. One-eighth inch material works well in the subtropical waters of Mexico.

Getting into your wetsuit is tricky. Various popular lubricants have disadvantages: talc can injure your lungs if breathed, cornstarch grows bacteria, and soap fragrances can warn fish of your presence long before you see them. Terry prefers a body lotion that contains no fragrances or oils. He mixes it half-and-half with water and sprays it into the suit. Avoid slippery shampoos near your feet—your feet can slip inside your boot or your fins can fall off.

You have two basic choices for the surface of your wetsuit: skin only (just the black smooth-rubber surface) or nylon-cloth coated. The nylon covering, while more expensive, offers several advantages. It's available in different colors and patterns, it's abrasion resistant, and for durability, it accepts seams that can be sewn. While a nylon suit is warmer under the water

than a skin suit, it becomes quite cold in the wind. If you dive from a boat, consider wearing a skin-only wetsuit or a slicker over an exposed nylon suit. Some manufacturers offer suits covered with a "plush" inner-lining. In our view, they're not worth the extra expense.

If you spear fish or take photographs, the color of your suit may be an important consideration. Don't mix colors on the same suit; the contrast is too easily detected by marine life. An all-black or a camouflage design works well for bottom fishing, while blue, green or silver is best for open water.

Those interested in depth records should consider using the skin-only exterior used by deep-diving enthusiasts. These suits employ glued rather than sewn seams to help decrease the coefficient of friction; this improves the laminar flow of water over the diver's body, which lets him glide faster. One Israeli manufacturer of these smooth suits says there may be a 10-percent decrease in friction over nylon-lined suits.

While neoprene is a rugged material, there are a few steps you can take to prolong the life of your wetsuit. Store your suit out of direct sunlight in a cool area to prevent premature hardening. Don't store it for too long in humid environments, such as the inside

Wear a vest under your wetsuit for added protection against the cold.

Dive skins offer modest protection from the cold and the sun. Worn under a wetsuit, they help prevent chafing.

"Shorty" wetsuits work well for brief dives in tropical waters.

of your divebag, which causes the fabric to separate from the rubber. Hang your wetsuit over broad-cushioned wetsuit hangers to distribute the weight and to prevent cracking at the pressure points.

Rinse your suit in fresh water after each use. When it gets smelly, rinse it in a vinegar solution—add a gallon of vinegar to a garbage can filled with water. Baking soda or a commercial "wetsuit shampoo" will work as well. Some sensitive divers develop skin infections, especially when they wear open-cell foam against their skin. To eliminate this problem, rinse the suit thoroughly after each use with an antibacterial soap, available from the drug store.

Use silicone, not petroleum jelly to lubricate the areas of your body prone to wetsuit chafe: around your neck, under your arms, and behind your knees and ankles. Petroleum jelly is a notorious wetsuit-glue solvent and will quickly dissolve the glue at the seams. Panty hose or dive skins, worn under your suit, will also prevent chafing.

In many warm-water regions—78 degrees or more (26 degrees Celsius)—dive skins offer the best protection against the sun, aquatic stinging creatures, sharp coral and the cold. Made from lycra, darylex or polartex, they are neutrally buoyant. Some dive skins produce warmth equivalent to a 3-millimeter wetsuit.

They require no offsetting lead weights and take up minimal baggage space.

WETSUIT ACCESSORIES

Important wetsuit accessories include pads, pouches, booties, gloves, hoods and vests.

You can apply custom pads and pouches to most flat surfaces of your wetsuit—chest, arms and legs. Commonly, divers carry knives and powerheads in the pouches. Streamlined pouches have the advantage of making items readily accessible and less likely to become involved in a deadly line-tangle.

Custom pads include back-pads, kneepads and speargun-loading pads. Kneepads cushion the knees of divers who use a knee-paddling technique for their paddleboard or kayak. Kneepads also protect against premature wetsuit wear for those divers who scrounge in the rocks for lobster, abalone, fish and photos.

An extra layer of material, glued onto the suit over the lower stomach, makes a useful speargun-cocking pad by distributing the loading force over a broad area. David learned the value of the cocking pad one summer. National Champion Mike McGuire

59

Boots and gloves protect you and keep you warm.

introduced a new speargun with massive 20-millimeter propulsion bands to David and North Atlantic Champion John Murphy. "We enthusiastically loaded and reloaded the aptly named, 110-pound-pull (50 kilogram), 'megaton' bands," David recalls. "Concentrating so much pressure through the single piece of rubber on our stomachs left us with red welts and bruises that lasted for days."

Wetsuit booties protect your feet and keep them warm. Make sure the seams run along the side of the boot and not the top, where they can chafe and erode skin. While thick-soled boots fit into open-pocket fins, they are unsuitable for full-pocket fins, which require a neoprene sock. Commonly made from material 1/8 to 3/16 inches (3 to 5 millimeters) thick, socks ensure a snug and comfortable fit, but the sole wears quickly. Shore divers entering over barnacle-covered rocks, or simply walking to their dive site will develop holes in their socks. It's not uncommon to replace two sets each season.

Terry devised a modification to his boots that enables them to survive several seasons intact. First, he fashions foot-inserts by cutting out each foot's outline from a scrap piece of wood 1/2- to 3/4-inch (1.3 to 2 centimeters) thick. He smooths the edges and labels them "L" and "R." After inserting the wood forms into his socks, he turns them up-side down and applies the tennis-shoe restorative "Shoe-goo" to the outside of the sole. He follows a thin layer covering the whole sole with a second, thicker layer over the heel and balls-of-the-feet area. When the Shoe-goo is dry and the sole is formed, he removes the wood inserts. The result-ing boots are quite durable and still retain enough flexibility to fit comfortably inside a full-pocket fin.

Gloves and mitts provide insulation and warmth. Most divers use 1/8 or 3/16-inch (3 or 5 millimeter) five-finger neoprene gloves. Gloves thicker than 3/16 inch (5 millimeters) are not practical because they are too stiff to allow adequate dexterity. Three-finger mitts are warmer than gloves and offer the ultimate in hand warmth. In warmer water, gloves made from neoprene and suede work well; the suede covers the gripping surface of the fingers and palm while neoprene covers the balance of the hand and wrist. Be sure to wear gloves when spearfishing; they protect your hands when you handle fish and load your gun.

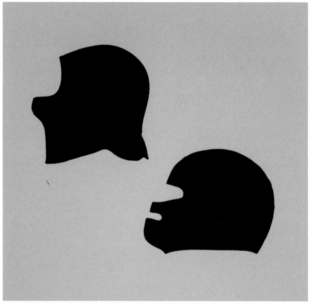

Because you can lose up to 20 percent of your body heat through your scalp, hoods are a good idea. Many wetsuits come with hoods attached.

Hoods prevent heat from escaping through your head—an area capable of radiating away a significant amount of your body heat. Ranked in descending order, from warmest to coldest, is the attached hood, the unattached hood with a bib or skirt and the simple hood without a bib. A typical northern, cold-water, unattached hood combines a 1/4-inch (6 millimeter) hood with an 1/8-inch (3-millimeter) bib that tucks under your jacket. The bib covers your neck and deflects water past the opening in the Farmer John.

You can mix and match wetsuits and accessories to meet your specific needs. For cold water, rather than using a stiff wetsuit made from material thicker than 1/4 inch (6 millimeters), consider adding an accessory. Vests and short pants enhance your wetsuit's warming

PHOTOS: COURTESY OF DEEP THOUGHT™

This diver demonstrates one principle of wetsuit layering for warmth. The wetsuit's patented belly seal helps keeps water out of this critical area.

potential. Worn under the wetsuit, they offer added insulation and form a second water seal. Sleeveless and legless, they allow for mobility while providing warmth to your trunk. Vests and short pants are made from thin material, 1/8 to 3/16 inches (3 to 5 millimeters) thick.

David uses a 3-millimeter full wetsuit for New England's summer waters. As the water cools in the fall, he adds a 3-millimeter vest. He switches to a full 1/4-inch (6-millimeter) suit in the winter and spring. Terry, when diving six hours a day in the 54-degree (12 degrees Celsius) water of Northern California, uses a full 1/4-inch wetsuit, a full 1/8- inch (3-millimeter) vest complete with arms and attached hood, 1/8-inch "hot pants" extending from just above the knee to the navel and two sets of gloves and boots.

Divers shed parts of their suit or wear shorter garments as the water becomes too warm for a complete suit. First, they might substitute their full pants for a shorter model cut off above the knee. Next, they would probably shed the pants and hood altogether, and last, they might wear a sleeveless jacket, or none at all. You might find yourself in water too warm for your suit and without a shorter suit to substitute. In that event, you can make your full wetsuit cooler by rolling up the sleeves at the wrists and the pant legs at the ankles and removing the hood. Easily repairable razor-cuts into the suit under the arms, in the crotch area and behind the neck will often allow sufficient circulation under the suit to make it bearable. Make one clean 3-inch (8-centimeter) cut at each location.

When selecting freediving wetsuits, warmth is a primary consideration. So is mobility, especially in the arms and chest. Selecting the correct accessory will help accomplish both goals.

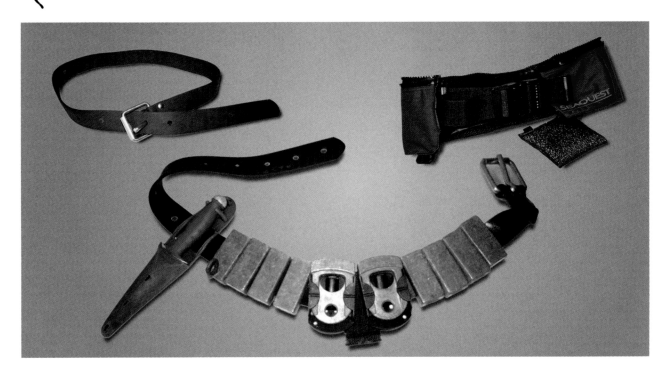

Your weight belt should have a quick-release buckle and a stretchable web with weights equally distributed.

WEIGHT BELTS

Weight belts are used to offset your body's natural tendency to float and the buoyancy of your wetsuit. A belt weighing 3 pounds (1.3 kilograms) is sufficient to neutralize the natural buoyancy of the average freediver not wearing a wetsuit. A 25-pound (11-kilogram) belt might not be enough for the diver wearing a full, cold-water wetsuit.

The two most important considerations regarding your weight belt are the quick-release mechanism and your **attitude** toward ditching the belt. The release mechanism needs to be durable and easily operable by either gloved hand. The best release mechanism will kill you if you don't use it early enough. When in doubt about reaching the surface, ditch your weight belt! Consider bringing along a cheap replacement belt and an aqua lung to help retrieve a lost belt.

Weight belts are available in several styles, colors and shapes. For safety, one might argue that the best belt is the least expensive because you would ditch it more readily in an emergency. Whatever style you choose, make sure you don't add too much weight—the belt must let you float upward in water 15-feet (4.5-meters) deep or less. This way, if you suffer shallow-water blackout at 15 feet, you will

float, which will increase your chances of surviving the accident.

Serious freedivers use a belt made from an elastic material—something that gently contracts around your waist to compensate for the compressive effects of water on both your body and wetsuit as you descend. It's frustrating to feel your belt slide down around your chest at 50 feet (15 meters).

The Marseilles-style weight belt, offered by many European manufacturers, is comfortable and durable. It's made from a 2-inch (5-centimeter) butyl-rubber strap and a large stainless-steel buckle. It compensates for chest and wetsuit compression at any depth. The buckle offers easy size adjustments and a quick-release mechanism for ditching.

You can make your own compensating belt by purchasing the rubber strap and a buckle from your specialty-dive shop. You can also modify a standard weight belt to compensate for stretch by burning a set of five parallel holes, an inch (2.5 centimeters) apart, into the web material not covered by weights. Finish the job by threading and fixing a 1/4-inch (3 millimeter) rubber bungee cord through the holes to form stretchable pleats.

Many freedivers suffer from some sort of back problem. For these people, a heavy weight belt that concentrates weight at the waist, places unacceptable pressure on their spine. To keep his belt low around his hips, Terry fashions a Velcro strap that connects the front and back of the weight belt through the crotch. This crotch-strap prevents any tendency of the belt to slip downward around the waist during descent into deep water.

Commercial abalone diver and Los Angeles champion Gary Thompson protects his back with a 10-inch (25-centimeter) wide belt cut from heavy, rubber conveyor-belt material. His weights, attached to the outside, distribute their force evenly over a large area of his lower back.

Another solution to the problem of weight distribution, popular in Australia and Europe, is the shoulder harness. Resembling a parachute harness, it's equipped with three quick-release buckles. The harness positions the diver's weights over his shoulders and upper back. Divers using this apparatus say that it takes some time to adapt to the weight shift from their waist to their upper back because the redistributed weight causes their head to sink deeper and makes their legs float higher. While this belt is comfortable for some divers, we worry about the feasibility of operating three separate release mechanisms in an emergency.

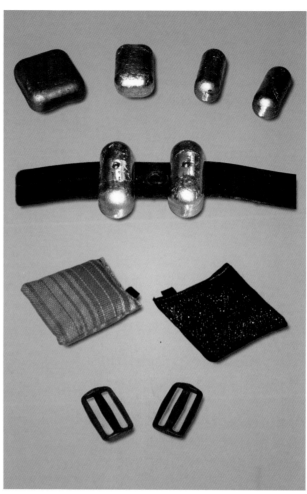

WEIGHTS

Lead weights for weight belts come in a variety of shapes and sizes. While square blocks and curved hip-weights are available, most freedivers prefer 2-pound (0.9 kilogram), bullet-shaped weights. They avoid sharp-edged weights that can dig into their back or sides. Whatever weights you choose, be sure that you distribute them evenly across the weight belt. Stainless-steel belt-spacers or set screws, imbedded into the weights, help keep the weights from shifting position on the belt.

Some lightweight weight belts employ lead shot. These comfortable and easily-adjustable belts work well for women and lighter individuals. The Velcro-equipped waist-belt accepts various-sized pouches that attach to the belt with double Velcro fasteners. To prevent the lead shot from solidifying and losing its flexibility, place it into Zip-Loc bags and rinse the shot occasionally.

Assorted weights and accessories: solid lead weights (top), lead-shot bags (middle) and plastic weight-belt weight retainers.

Some divers use special accessory weights on their legs, attached to their fins or clasped around their ankles. They're useful for fin-swimming training or for shallow-water hunting because they help keep surface splashing to a minimum. People with bad backs appreciate the weight reduction from their waist-belt and photographers prefer legs that hug the bottom. But leg weights have their drawbacks, too: the leg weights can cause ankle abrasions and contribute to fatigue by increasing the drag-producing profile.

One manufacturer offers a modular system that uses weight receivers that allow you to rapidly adjust your weights in the water. Users exchange weights from their belts to their fins by simply unsnapping and snapping them between locations.

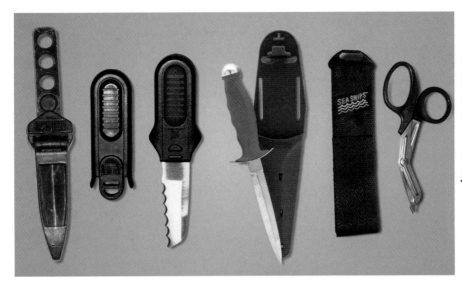

Knives and shears. Note the compact size. The two knives on the left are equipped with quick-removal mechanisms. You'll need shears if you dive near fishing line or wrecks.

A pouch, mounted onto your wetsuit, is an excellent way to carry your knife. Be sure that you can reach your knife with either hand.

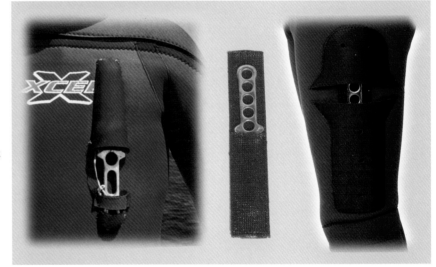

KNIVES AND SHEARS

Knives are important safety equipment. Freedivers use them to cut entangled line and as a last defense against sharks. Spearfishers use them to dispatch and field-dress their catch. The best knife is small and sharp and has a comfortable grip. It should be held in its sheath by a mechanical lock or a rubber keeper; you must be able to operate either mechanism while wearing gloves.

Where you place your knife and attach it to your body are important safety considerations. It should be equally accessible to either hand. Divers commonly carry their knives on their legs, arms, chest, weight belt and, sometimes, speargun. Don't carry the knife on your leg because it will interfere with kicking and be vulnerable to line tangles. Your weight belt is a good

location for your knife because, if a line should tangle around the knife-sheath, you can ditch it easily by dropping the weight belt. You should locate the knife near the middle of the belt so you can reach it with either hand.

Terry prefers to carry his knife on his chest. He places the knife in a neoprene-rubber pouch, handle down, where it's streamlined and accessible to both hands. He attaches a small lanyard to the handle to catch the knife should it be accidentally dislodged or dropped.

You should also consider carrying stainless-steel shears if you dive near breakwaters or close to fishermen. Fishing line and thin stainless-steel leaders used by fishermen can be deadly for the freediver unequipped to cut them quickly.

FLOATS, FLAGS AND LINES

Floats and flags are indispensable freediving gear. An adequate float can be as simple as a blow-up buoy or as complicated as a mini-surfboard. Floats help transport your flag and other accessories such as food, flashlights, game-bags and spearfishing gear. Besides supporting the "divers-down" flag, they should be able to float you or a buddy in an emergency.

Some divers find that a boogie board makes a serviceable float. These firm, flexible, foam boards handle well, provide a suitable resting platform and are capable of carrying extra equipment.

Riffe International manufactures an excellent inflatable float. Made of heavy, 210-denier nylon, it's designed to follow a speared fish hundreds of feet deep and retain some buoyancy—20 pounds at 100 feet (9 kilos at 30 meters). The 3-pound weight (1.3 kilo), positioned at the bottom of the float, keeps the divers-down flag upright. Two small elastic tubes hold stringers or flares, and the float's bright-orange color is very visible in choppy seas. The float's torpedo-like shape makes it easy to tow.

Divers-down flags are required in many countries and should be a part of every freediver's gear. The purpose of the flag is to signal others, particularly boaters, that divers are in the water. Flags may be flown from a boat, an anchored kayak or towed on the diver's float. Local laws may specify the maximum distance divers are permitted to swim away from their floats and a minimum distance for how close boats may approach—typically 50 to 100 feet (15 to 30 meters). The blue-and-white "alpha flag" is the internationally recognized diver's flag. In the United States, the flag is red and white. Many divers carry both.

Since state and international laws vary concerning the size of the flag, its height and the number of divers allowed per flag, you need to consult local laws for the specifics. Proper display of your flag, according to local laws, is imperative to prevent boats from running you over. But beware: the flag does not guarantee your safety. Curious boaters, ignorant of the flag's meaning, sometimes drive their craft close to flagged buoys, perhaps to take them, while other boaters have used flagged buoys as waterski pylons!

Placing a flag atop a buoy also helps locate divers lost at sea. Without a flag, it's easy for observers to lose track of a diver's whereabouts in rough, choppy seas. A good float and flag can be spotted from a much greater distance than a diver's head bobbing on the surface.

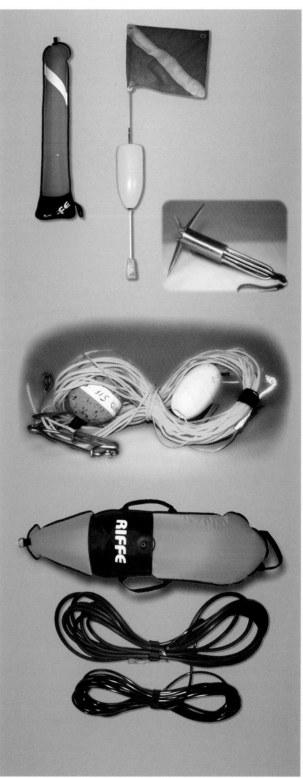

Diver's floats, flag, lines and anchor.

A kayak offers an excellent freediving platform.

Four kayaks and a paddleboard (right) provide stable and economical transportation for near-shore divers.

Many competitive divers use paddleboards because they ride low in the water—out of the wind. Racing divers propel these boards with both arms and legs.

PHOTOS: RON MULLINS

Because of the potential hazard of a line tangle, you should consider your choice of a tow-line carefully; it should float and it should not be so thin that it tangles or knots easily. Ranked in order of least expensive to most expensive: (1) a 1/8-inch (3 millimeter) polypropylene line; (2) a line made with parachute-cord running inside a clear vinyl tube; and (3) for the serious spearfisher, a long and stretchable 1/2-inch (13-millimeter) neoprene tube with parachute-cord laced inside. Both kinds of tubes are sealed at each end with metal plugs that are fitted with swivels and quick-release clips. Tubes are easy to grab, they seldom kink or nest and they are less likely to cause a dangerous half-hitch knot to bind one of your arms or legs.

DIVE BOARDS AND KAYAKS

Dive boards and wet-bottomed kayaks are gaining popularity among today's divers. The diving-instruction organization PADI has even sanctioned a kayak-dive class. Dive boards and kayaks provide you with transportation, a place to store your equipment and game, and a good support for your divers-down flag. These inexpensive alternatives to boats offer the pleasure of paddling and the opportunity to condition your upper body.

Dive boards expand the shore-diver's horizons by at least 20 times. The San Diego Bottom Scratchers recognized their utility in the late 1930s. Jack Prodonovich felt that there had to be a better alternative to his inner-tube float. This was well before the introduction of the wetsuit, and Jack, who was thin and fit, got cold just kicking his inner tube to his dive site beyond the surf.

Jack's first paddleboard, made in 1936, is still quite sophisticated by today's standards. He cut a 10-foot (3-meter) long piece of plywood into the outline of an elongated surfboard. For depth and contour, he then placed ribs on its bottom and covered them with canvas—not unlike an old-fashioned airplane wing. His finishing touch was a through-and-through hole, cut out for his face, exposing the water below. When paddling, he placed his facemask into the well, which gave him a high-speed preview of the reefs.

During the forties, fifties and early sixties, most freedivers used elongated surfboards for transportation. To the tops of these solid filled boards, they fashioned elaborate racks for the attachment of gear and for the storage of game. In the late 1960s, Steve Ryan of Oregon introduced the forerunner of the modern fiberglass paddleboard. Fourteen feet (11-meters) long, the hollow board sported a graceful upswept nose for surf penetration, knee wells for hand-paddling and a large forward compartment, complete with a latched cover, for storage. In calm water, you could propel it by using canoe-like paddles from a seated position. When the water was rough, you laid with your chest on the compartment lid and used your arms in a normal surfboard stroke or your finned legs in a modified frog-kick stroke or, if you were in a hurry, you used both methods. Paddleboards are still used in most United States National Spearfishing Championships.

Besides being an excellent emergency platform, a kayak offers watertight compartments for flotation and storage. In the mid-eighties the designs of paddleboards and kayaks converged when Mallate Manufacturing introduced its fiberglassed, wet-bottomed kayak, the "Scuba Scout." Today, Ocean Kayak and Aqua Terra make good kayaks suitable for freedivers.

An important freediving accessory is an anchor and anchor line. A 5-pound (2.3 kilogram) anchor, attached to a 10-foot (3-meter) length of thick-stainless wire cable or thin chain, and tied to 80 feet (24 meters) of line, works well. Keep the anchor line coiled on a line keeper to prevent nasty snags and tangles. California divers carry a 15-foot (4.5 meter) line connected to a harness snap for temporary anchoring to kelp beds; they wrap the line several times around a few kelp stalks and secure it with the snap. Some divers have added small bilge pumps to remove unwanted water encroaching from rough seas. If you plan to use a kayak, be sure to check local laws for such requirements as life vests and registration.

Compared to the gear required for many other sports, freediving equipment is relatively inexpensive—surely an appealing aspect of this sport. However, because of the potential dangers associated with freediving, you must make a special effort to choose gear that is both functional and safe.

A mother humpback whale with her new baby off Maui.

Technique

Soft, smooth, quiet, confident, serene, peaceful: all these adjectives hint at the intense pleasure well-trained freedivers feel. Imagine coasting below the waves, playing "pass the leaf" with wild dolphins, flying in formation with giant manta rays or simply joining a school of fish. Without a mechanical breathing apparatus, you're truly free—free to flow effortlessly into the womb-like, enveloping water, free to join the ocean not as an interloper but as a welcome friend.

Lying at the surface face down, you take slow, deep, quiet breaths. Your body is totally relaxed, your mind open and free of anxiety. Gently sealing your nose, you pre-equalize your ears. While kicking lightly to give yourself some forward momentum, you simultaneously take your last full-capacity breath, flood your snorkel, bend at the waist and raise one of your legs. Without making a splash, you leave the surface in a perfect inverted dive.

Slow, streamlined kicks propel you until gravity overcomes buoyancy and you glide downward—effortlessly. Multiple, frequent ear-clearings help prevent ear discomfort.

Seconds later, you feel the bottom approaching and a flash catches your eye. To slow your descent, you raise your head and slightly part your fins. The flash materializes into a single fish swimming toward you. Wishing to continue your glide to the bottom, you tuck your head downward and close your legs and aim for a perfect landing.

After a graceful stop, you suddenly find yourself swarmed by colorful reef fish. Slowly scanning side-to-side, you notice a larger fish in the distance—cautiously but curiously watching you. With your finger tips you push off the bottom and initiate a glide toward another observation post on the reef.

Schooling fish separate their formation for your passage and then fill in behind you. Before feeling the urge to breathe, you begin your slow ascent back to the surface. To pierce the water column above, you adopt a streamlined kicking form—legs together with your hands folded at your groin. Just before reaching the surface, you exhale water-displacing air into your snorkel. Breaking the surface, you quench your thirsty lungs with fresh air.

Congratulations! You just made a perfect freedive.

Freediving is a sport most people with basic swimming skills can master. Since we define freediving as holding your breath an inch or more underwater, most snorkelers already qualify.

We'll begin this chapter with the basics: your attitude and how to use your gear. Next, we'll take you through a series of pool exercises—fin swimming, cramp management, surface dives, ear clearing—and then we'll graduate to open water. The chapter ends with advanced training techniques and examines common freediving accidents.

How should you learn freediving? Not like the newlyweds we observed in Hawaii. The young man coaxed his new bride into the water, assuring her she had nothing to fear. Timidly she placed the unfamiliar snorkel into her mouth, flip-flopped to the reef's edge and jumped in. In the water, she bicycled furiously with finned feet, clawed the water with her arms and made a brave attempt to look into the surging water before declaring, "I can't!"

What happened? Unfamiliar with the equipment, uncomfortable in the horizontal position, and hammered by the heart-racing cold and fear of

BASIC POOL EXERCISES

Since comfort in the water is the key to freediving, let's start with a simple, yet effective, relaxation maneuver—the "floating fetal position." (If you're not familiar with how to use a snorkel or mask, skip ahead to those sections and then return to this exercise.)

Exercise 1: The floating fetal position. Locate a warm swimming pool or a calm clear body of water approximately 10 feet (3 meters) deep. For your first lesson, choose the most pressure-free time of the week—that's Saturday morning for most people. Put on your gear and float face down. Breathe gently through your snorkel. Curl into the fetal position and then relax.

Let your limbs go limp and fall where they may. Breathe slowly and regularly. You should be free of anxiety or muscle tension. Say these words in your

Exercise 1: The floating fetal position

animals lurking at her feet, she panicked. Remember, freediving is about familiarity, ease, relaxation and energy conservation.

To learn to freedive, find a competent, patient instructor who will guide you through the selection of your gear and introduce you to the basic elements of the sport in a step-wise, confidence-building fashion. This chapter is not intended to be a teach-yourself program. While we have numbered each exercise, your instructor should select both the exercises and their order of introduction into your unique training program. Avoid advancing until you're competent with the last step.

mind: "soft" "smooth" and "quiet." You'll know the exercise is working when you feel that you could fall asleep. This is the same feeling that trained freedivers have, whether they're on the surface preparing for a dive or 60 feet underwater photographing an elusive sea creature.

To lengthen the duration of your dives, you must learn the essence of freediving—a heightened level of mental and sensory awareness coupled with a body that is so relaxed it's almost asleep. This exercise and the resulting mind state is so important that you should begin every training session with it. This is your baseline; it's the feeling you must always be able to summon. Since this exercise depends in part on comfortable gear, we'll discuss the use of basic freediving gear before continuing with your pool training.

Exercise 2: Mouth-breathing with the snorkel

Your snorkel

You must master the snorkel in the initial stages of training. Freedivers breathe exclusively through their mouths. For most of us, mouth-breathing is uncomfortable at first. Normally, the only time we breathe through our mouths is when our noses are congested.

Exercise 2: Mouth-breathing with the snorkel. At the pool's edge, place your snorkel in your mouth and become familiar with breathing through it before you enter the water. Next, stand in waist-deep water and bend over with your face in the water. Continue to breathe until you feel comfortable.

Your snorkel's greatest value is that it affords you an uninterrupted view of the water below. To obtain this view, you must lie on the surface horizontally and in the face-down position—a position that except when you're sleeping, can be mighty uncomfortable. If you've ever watched an uncoached beginning freediver like our newlywed, you'll see someone struggling to remain vertical, usually by thrashing the water with his or her fins and arms. Your goal should be to enter the water feeling relaxed and confident in the horizontal position. Your arms should be still and your legs should generate slow, graceful kicks.

Exercise 3: Breathing horizontally. Hold your snorkel in your mouth with one hand, and use the other hand to hold on to the edge of the pool as you float horizontally. Without a mask, place your face in the water and breathe. Practicing this exercise without your mask teaches control of your upper airway when you close your nose and breathe through your mouth. Try closing your eyes and focusing on the touch of the water and the pool side and the sounds of the pool equipment. Once you are comfortable with breathing you can practice snorkel clearing.

It's an unavoidable fact that, when freediving, water will occasionally make its way into your snorkel. Some manufacturers capitalize on this problem by equipping their snorkels with a bewildering array of valves that promise to keep water out or to make water exit easily. You don't need the valves. With a little experience, you'll learn to sense water entering your snorkel in plenty of time to stop your breath. You'll learn how to slowly breathe air to bypass accumulated water in the snorkel's "J" and then blast it out with a quick blow—the "blast method."

Exercise 3: Breathing horizontally

Exercise 4: Snorkel clearing by blast. Submerge your head and snorkel. Listen to and feel the water fill your snorkel. Then slowly begin to stand up. When you feel the top of your head and the snorkel at the surface, blow forcefully into your snorkel to clear the water

Exercise 4: Snorkel clearing by blast

inside. Now take a slow, deep breath. If there is any remaining water in the snorkel, you may hear a gurgling sound. Don't be alarmed. Simply continue to inhale slowly and then exhale forcefully to remove that excess water. Whenever you sense water inside your snorkel, don't attempt a quick inhalation since this may cause you to bring the water into your mouth and throat.

Once you are comfortable with snorkel clearing, attach your snorkel to your mask. Your snorkel must fit passively and comfortably in your mouth—rather than push, bind or dig into your gums. Slide it up and down, through the snorkel retainer, until it's comfortable. Position the snorkel so that when you are horizontally facing into the water, it's vertical in the air.

Exercise 5: Snorkel clearing by displacement. Most freedivers clear their snorkels of water when they surface by the "displacement method" which is easier to use, more quiet and takes less energy.

Lie on the bottom of the shallow end of the pool and pause for a few seconds. Now swim towards the surface and level off about 6 to 10 inches (15 to 25 centimeters) under the surface. Your snorkel should be pointing generally upward. Gently exhale into your snorkel. Rising air inside the snorkel does all the work for you. As it bubbles upward, it pushes the water upward and out of the snorkel. Because you don't need to exhale forcefully, this technique is relatively quiet.

Exercise 5: Snorkel clearing by displacement

We recommend that you keep your snorkel in your mouth throughout the dive. Divers who spit their snorkels out must replace them at the surface after each dive. This is a waste of effort, and it's difficult to manage if your hands are occupied with cameras or game. Freedivers generally remove their snorkels for two reasons: bubbling from the snorkel on descent and jaw pain. You can stop noisy air from bubbling out of your snorkel by opening your mouth slightly at the surface when you begin your surface dive—wide enough to let water in but not so wide that the snorkel falls out. Water filling your snorkel through your mouth displaces the air as you submerge to prevent bubbles.

For jaw comfort, consider a custom-fitted mouthpiece. Check your snorkel's tooth grips for signs of excessive tension. Some beginners, uneasy about freediving, transfer their worries to their jaw muscles. If there is evidence that you're biting through the teeth pads, it's time to revisit the basic relaxation exercises.

Your mask

Try tucking your mask on instead of "putting" it on. Simply putting (placing) a mask on your face stretches your skin under the flange seal; when your stretched skin moves under the mask, it breaks the seal and the mask leaks. But when you tuck your mask on your face, you bring in extra skin under the mask to assist the seal when you move. To tuck your mask on, bring the mask to your face, close your eyes and pull down your upper lip so that the mask flange seats under your nose cartilage. Seating the mask in this fashion captures some stretchable skin under the seal to compensate for movement. Test the mask seal without using the strap. A sniff of air should hold the mask onto your face when you lean over. Position the straps just above the tips of your ears. Straps should be snug, not tight, because water pressure alone will keep the mask on your face. If you develop "mask ring-around-the-face," your straps are too tight.

In the world freediving championships in Italy, Terry learned about the effects of facial-muscle tension on mask leakage. His custom-built mask, which conforms exactly to the contours of his face, leaked during the first half-hour of the meet. It had not leaked before and it has not leaked since. Apparently, the excitement of the contest translated into facial-muscle tension—enough to break the mask's seal to his skin. After the initial half-hour passed, he calmed enough so that his facial muscles relaxed and the mask fit again.

Laughter frequently floods your mask as well. If you're relaxed enough to laugh underwater, you're surely competent enough to clear your mask.

Classical scuba instructors teach the mask-clearing maneuver by replacing a water-flooded mask space with compressed air. While this maneuver may not appear to be practical for freedivers, who have a limited air supply, intentionally flooding the mask teaches control and familiarity with a water-filled or lost mask. Practice surfacing with a flooded mask and no mask at all. Become comfortable with blurred vision—or in the case of contact wearers, no vision at all—and finding your way back to the surface. Practice swimming with your arms outstretched in front of you to prevent hitting your head on surface objects such as the bottom of your boat or a buoy. Should you lose your mask in deep water and become disoriented, dump your weight belt and follow the direction of your bubbles to the surface.

During a competition, freediver John Murphy flooded his mask and attempted to clear it. When he opened his eyes, he still couldn't see. After several attempts to clear his mask at a depth of approximately 25 feet (7.5 meters) in water with 3 feet (1 meter) of visibility, he began his ascent. When he arrived at the surface, he found that both of his lenses had fallen out of the mask. Miraculously, he found both lenses on his next dive on the reef without the mask. This is a fine example of a diver completely adjusted to the underwater environment through good training.

Exercise 6: Mask clearing. Practice clearing your mask above water before attempting it underwater. Begin this exercise standing in shallow water. With your mask on your face, simply bend over and flood it, and then return to your standing position. Tilt your head back slightly as if to look straight up in the air. Place one hand on top of your mask and gently press in. This will break the mask's seal above your upper lip. Gently and continually exhale air from your nose into the mask. You need not lift the mask off your face—just break the lower seal. Your goal is to replace the water

Exercise 6: Mask clearing

with air. Once the water is gone, remove the pressure from the top of the mask and allow the skirt to settle back on your face, stop your exhalation and open your eyes.

Now try this technique underwater. Kneel down in water just deep enough to cover your head. If you have trouble staying under, have your partner hold you down by the shoulders (with a pre-arranged signal for release). Flood your mask by breaking the upper seal, not the lower. This prevents water from gushing up into your nose from below. Once the mask is flooded, repeat the steps described above.

Many new divers mistakenly exhale through their mouths instead of their noses, or lift their masks off of their faces instead of just breaking the lower seal.

Practice until the level of water in the mask lowers slowly, without the loss of extra bubbles from under the mask skirt.

Managing a foggy faceplate

When your mask lens is dirty, water fogs your faceplate and obscures your vision. To prevent this condition, clean a newly purchased faceplate thoroughly by scouring it with toothpaste on a cotton ball. The silicone-grease lens coating, common to new masks, is quite adherent and takes about 15 minutes to eliminate. Just before you dive, spit into the mask, smear it around and then rinse it out. Pre-treatment with commercial anti-fog faceplate treatments also works well. If none of the above is available, try scrubbing your mask with a piece of seaweed. At the end of the day, be sure to wash off your mask with soap and water; this cleans the lens and removes blemish-forming bacteria from the skirt.

Spitting into your mask helps keeps it fog-free.

Your fins

Choose flexible fins and wear socks or rubber booties for protection against foot chafing and ulcers. The foot pocket should fit firmly without causing pressure points or cramping. Your feet should not slide inside the fin when you shake your foot up and down or side to side.

Like our young honeymooner, many beginners tend to flex their knees deeply and appear to "bicycle" through the water. They often make large and unnecessary arm and hand movements. Remember, keep your hands relaxed at your side. Flailing arms and excessive knee flexing waste your valuable energy, cause efficiency-robbing drag through the water and make a lot of noise, which scares away marine life. When you kick, use your hip and knee joints equally. If you flex your knee too much (bicycling), loosely wrap your knee joint with a bandage as a reminder to use straight-legged kicking from your hip. Be sure to keep your feet below the water when you swim on the surface.

Before graduating to open-water training, you should master three fin-kicking strokes: the basic slow-flutter kick, the frog kick and the dolphin kick. You'll use the basic slow-flutter kick stroke about 90 percent of the time. Keep the strokes even and smooth. Kick gently, don't overpower the fins and keep the blades in the same plane as your leg stroke to prevent water from "spilling off" the side of the fin.

Because of the flexible and elastic nature of freediving fins, it's important that you understand how they work. As you kick, your fins produce forward motion when the blades displace water backwards. Additionally, the fin blade's natural recoil provides some propulsion.

Take a fin in both hands, hold it lengthwise, flex the blade about 30 to 45 degrees and note how the blade's recoil snaps the fin back to its horizontal position when you release the blade. Visualize how the blade pushes water behind it and how the blade's recoil contributes to the fin's efficiency. Now, overpower the fin by bending the blade 90 degrees. See how water must spill off the blade ineffectually, and note the reduction in elastic recoil when you release the blade. The goal of the following fin exercises is to help you maintain your fin strokes within the optimal range and to help you develop a smooth fin stroke.

Exercise 7: Fin control vertical. Position yourself vertically in the water and note the water level on your mask. Start flutter kicking smoothly and gently but strongly enough to lower the water level about an inch as you rise out of the water. You'll know your kicking strokes are smooth and regular when the water level stays even.

To apply more power efficiently to your fins, increase the rate of your stride, not the amount of fin deflection. Think of a fleeing fish; when it's frightened, its tail beats at a faster pace, not a broader stroke. Test this by raising out of the water so your chin becomes level with the water. Next, kick faster to lower the water level to your chest. Remember to keep the strokes

The flutter kick: note the angle of the knees and ankles and the degree of fin deflection.

smooth so that the water level does not fluctuate. For fun, try to maintain the highest level out of the water you can for several seconds and test which fin stroke works best. Overpower the fin with broad powerful strokes and note how your level in the water falls.

Repeat the vertical fin exercises with your eyes closed. While you maintain a smooth kicking stroke, concentrate on sensing and feeling the water around you.

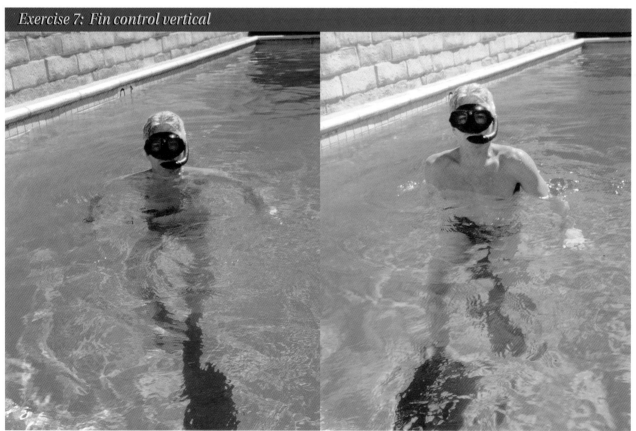

Exercise 7: Fin control vertical

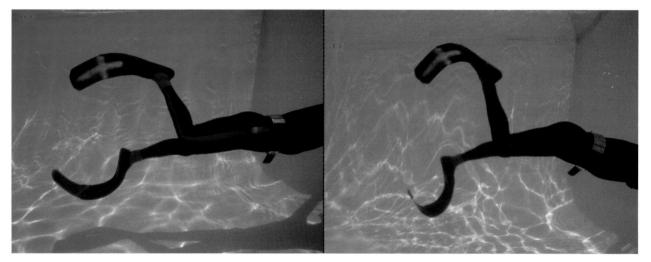

National Freediving Champion Bill Ernst demonstrates maximal deflection of the fins for power.

Here, Bill shows how "overkicking" reduces the fin's efficiency.

Exercise 8: Fin control horizontal. To develop horizontal control of your fins, grasp the pool edge with one hand, float horizontally and brace yourself against the pool with your other hand. Develop a smooth, narrow kicking stroke. Evaluate your form by looking back at your fins. Repeat this exercise in the middle of the pool by attaching a firm bungee cord, stretched across the pool to your weight belt. This rubber-bungee mechanism is an excellent way to practice all fin strokes in the confined setting of the swimming pool.

For the first part of the kick, keep your fins flat and slide them sideways and outward underwater in a non-thrust producing stroke. Now, for thrust, tilt your fins inward like a sculler and bring them together. Learn to make a smooth transition from the outward to the inward stroke. This is an ideal kick to help you maintain your position over the bottom in water moving with a slight current.

Exercise 8: Fin control horizontal

Exercise 9: Frog kick

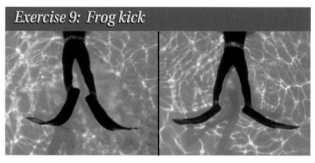

Exercise 9: Frog kick. Since the frog kick uses different muscles than the flutter, it is a good alternative when you are tired and need to rest your flutter muscles.

Exercise 10: Dolphin kick. The dolphin kick is the fastest fin stroke you can make in the water but it's also the most tiring. (Refer to the chapter on monofins for a special variation of the dolphin stroke used exclusively by monofin swimmers.) While you might go 30 percent faster underwater with this stroke, you'll burn at least 30 percent more energy. Use this stroke when you require a brief burst of speed or when your flutter muscles are fatigued. It is the most common alternative to the flutter kick.

Exercise 10: Dolphin kick

Keep your hands out front or at your sides and your fins together as you pivot at your pelvis. Thrust your pelvis down for one stroke and raise your buttocks for the other. This causes your body to undulate, just like marine mammals. Since your body is longer from the waist back, you'll have more motion at your fins than at your head. Remember, once again, don't overpower the fins.

Exercise 11: Cramp release. Cramps are caused by poor physical conditioning, fatigue, dehydration, cold water or an ill-fitting fin. Some cramps are so severe that they can immobilize and debilitate you. Most cramps occur in your calf or in the sole of your foot.

Exercise 11: Cramp release

Practice relieving cramps in the water by pulling on the tip of your fin blade (or the middle if you can't reach the tip) while keeping your leg straight. This position stretches your calf. Self massage or assistance from your dive buddy helps release the tightened muscles. Prevent cramps by stretching your leg muscles before you dive. If cramps reoccur, try another kicking technique.

Your weight belt

By selecting the appropriate weights, you'll dive more safely and gracefully. You'll exert less effort and have more fun. Properly weighted underwater, you'll resemble the weightless astronaut—just a small fin thrust propels you a long way. As your air-consuming, noisy motions decrease, your opportunities for interactions with underwater life increase. You'll cause less wear-and-tear on both your body and the environment.

Rig your belt so that you distribute the weights evenly. Use special weight belt slide-retainers to help prevent weights from shifting or falling off the end of the belt. Wear your belt around your hips, not your waist. Concentrating your weights around your waist causes excessive stress on your vulnerable lower back, and the belt interferes with abdominal breathing.

As a general rule, you'll want to weight yourself for the depth you plan to dive—you should neither sink nor float at that depth. To get an estimate of the proper weight to use, float vertically in the water, release half a breath and note the level of the water on your face plate. If the water is level with your eyes, your weight is close to ideal.

In shallow water, less than 10 feet (3 meters) deep, adjust your weights so that you remain floating after you completely exhale. If you exhale and sink, remove a pound or two and try again. Positive buoyancy at the surface helps you relax as you take deep, slow breaths in preparation for your dive.

Because your lungs and wetsuit compress with depth, you'll need less weight as you dive deeper. A 6.5-millimeter wetsuit provides 24 pounds (10.9 kilograms) of buoyancy at the surface. It loses 12 pounds (5.4 kilograms) of buoyancy at 33 feet (10 meters) and it loses 16 pounds (7.3 kilograms) at 66 feet (20 meters).

The most important test of your weight is that you should definitely float to the surface from water 15 feet (4.5 m) deep, the depth at which most shallow-water blackout occurs. Freedivers do not wear scuba buoyancy compensators (life jacket-like affairs) because they are bulky, they trap air and they are impractical since there is no air source available to inflate them. If you need buoyancy in an emergency, dump your belt!

Ear clearing

Remember, for successful ear clearing, clear early, often and gently. Don't force clearing and don't dive with a cold. To enhance ear clearing on the day of your dive, consider preparing your ears several days in advance. If you are at the tail end of a cold, with the advice of your physician, consider the use of antihistamines and decongestants. These drugs are designed to dry up secretions and open blocked eustachian tubes. Remember, however, that when these drugs wear off they can contribute to reverse ear block, as we discussed in the second physiology chapter.

Condition your eustachian tubes by pre-inflating them the day or two before diving. Seal the bottom of your nose and blow until both eardrums pop. Instead of immediately releasing the pressure, as you normally would while freediving, keep the pressure on for 10 to 20 seconds. You'll probably feel uncomfortable and a little dizzy. Repeat eustachian tube inflation several times throughout the day.

You can use several methods to "equalize" or clear your ears: blow against your nose, swallow, reposition your tongue or use various combinations of these movements. Learn as many methods as possible before you decide which one works best for you.

With any method, equalize at the surface before you dive and every 2 to 3 feet (0.6 to 1 meter) throughout your descent. If you feel pain or any discomfort, stop the descent and try equalizing again. If you can't clear, you may have to ascend a few feet. If you still can't clear, abort the dive and try another in a few minutes. To avoid serious ear injury, never force equalization. Quit diving for the day.

Don't confuse the normal ear-clearing sounds of crackling and popping with a problem clearing your ears. Unless these sounds are accompanied by pain, they are the normal sounds made by air moving through your eustachian tubes as they open and close intermittently.

The Valsalva maneuver is probably the most common ear-clearing method used by freedivers. Seal your nostrils, then seal your snorkel with your tongue and blow gently into your nose. The pressure you generate forces air from your throat through the eustachian tubes into the middle ear cavity to equalize pressure on both sides of the eardrum.

Although the Valsalva maneuver is the most common means of equalizing the middle ear, you should know that it can provoke short-term physiological changes in some individuals—irregular heart beat and high or low blood pressure. Fortunately, this is a rare occurrence. However, if you suffer from heart or blood pressure problems, obtain your physician's consent before you use this maneuver.

In some instances, the Valsalva is associated with nose bleeds, particularly in cold water. If this happens to you, reevaluate your technique. David finds that during open water instruction, some students forcefully pinch their nose rather than gently sealing their nostrils. Rough pinching ruptures blood vessels lining the inside of your nose. Refer to the physiology section on sinus squeeze since this condition may also cause a nosebleed.

A safer option is the Frenzel maneuver, originally developed for aviators. Seal your nose and thrust the back portion of your tongue upward. Notice that your adam's apple moves up and down and your nostrils may flare.

Another option is the Toynbee maneuver. Seal your nose, close your mouth, place your tongue up against the roof of your mouth and swallow—much like removing peanut butter from the top of your mouth. Some may find the Toynbee maneuver does not work well, especially if they have difficulty swallowing with a snorkel in their mouth. This method is generally not useful in rapid descents because there is little chance that a successful second attempt will follow a failed first try.

The Lowry technique is a combination of the Toynbee and Valsalva. Seal your nostrils, then swallow and blow at the same time. Although this sounds confusing at first, you'll catch on quickly. Try to learn each individual maneuver before you attempt to combine them.

The expert freediver learns to clear his ears easily by developing control over a certain group of muscles in his throat that assist the opening of the eustachian tubes. This is the same muscle group that moves with the other muscles in you head and neck when you swallow or perform exaggerated jaw and tongue movements. When you apply pressure to your nose, control over this special group of muscles bypasses the need to swallow or move your jaw in an attempt to clear your ears.

Exercise 12: Ear clearing

The primary muscles in this group are referred to as the Tensor veli palatini and the Levator veli palatini (the elevators of your soft palate). When you swallow, your jaw, tongue, adam's apple and soft palate (the soft back part of the roof of your mouth where a tissue tag dangles into your throat) all move upward. It's not necessary for your tongue or jaw to move for ear clearing—just your soft palate and adam's apple.

To visualize how these muscles work, stand in front of a well-lighted mirror with your mouth open. Now swallow, but try to keep your jaw and tongue as still as possible. When you master this maneuver, only your soft palate and adam's apple will move upward, and your ears should pop. If you don't hear the pop, try pre-inflating your eustachian tubes and repeat the maneuver. If the pressure in your ears releases, you've learned how to control these muscles.

The reward for learning this maneuver is that you may be able to clear your ears hands-free. If you can adapt your nose pocket to seal your nasal openings and then use this muscle group, you'll clear all the way to the bottom.

Exercise 12: Ear clearing. Using any of the above ear-clearing methods, start at the surface and continually clear to a depth of 10 feet (3 meters) to 12 feet (4 meters). Your goal is to clear frequently and completely so that you feel no pain.

The surface dive

Every freedive begins at the surface. It's important to enter the water smoothly and efficiently. In one fluid motion, you'll hold your last breath, bend at the waist and slip into the water. Like a spring-board diver scoring a perfect 10, you should leave behind barely a ripple of water.

Exercise 13: Surface dive. After resting on the surface long enough to flush out carbon dioxide and to replenish your lungs with oxygen, you're ready to start your surface-dive exercise. You should feel completely relaxed; your breathing rate should be slow and regular. Your breaths should be somewhat deeper than normal—at least 150 cubic centimeters (a half-cup of air) to cancel the effects of the extra, snorkel-induced, dead-space air.

Progressively increase the depth and rate of your last three breaths, starting with a relaxed breath and progressing to the deepest breath you're capable of drawing. Remember to make full use of your diaphragm. For your last breath, forcefully exhale to the maximum and then fill your lungs to capacity. During these last breaths, simultaneously pre-equalize your ears and initiate forward momentum by using either a flutter or a frog kick. Forward motion helps improve your surface entry.

At the moment your lungs fill, break your body at the waist, raise your left leg to the vertical position and bring your right hand up to the nose-sealing position on your mask by making a smooth "S" pattern with your arm. Slip your hand sideways through the water to minimize water resistance.

Three to five full kicking strokes should get you to the neutral point (where you neither sink nor float), after which little, if any, kicking is required to continue the descent.

The sensation of falling through the water is a good indication that you have made a perfect surface entry. If you find yourself struggling to get below the

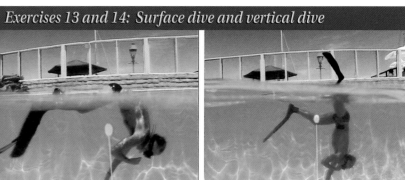

VIDEO CLIP: *The Joy of Freediving* BY TERRY MAAS AND LASZLO PAL.

Bill performs a perfect, vertical surface dive.

surface, chances are that you're not entering vertically. A less-than-vertical dive exposes the large drag-inducing surface of your chest to the water, rather than your streamlined finger tips and head. Sometimes, however, spearfishers use a flat-angle dive to get a good view of the mid-water fish.

It is not necessary to raise both legs—one leg provides sufficient downward force. The other leg aids stability at the start of the tuck and is in a good position to start your first kick when you're vertical and your fin tips clear the surface.

To get an idea of the vertical force your raised leg imparts to your downward momentum, try this exercise on your bed: Lie on your stomach and slide your upper body horizontally off the bed so that the lower half of your rib cage is at the bed's edge. Simultaneously, lower your right arm and raise your left leg as described above. You'll feel a considerable force driving you to the floor—it's the same motion that propels you into the water.

Exercise 14: Vertical dive. A good pool exercise to encourage a vertical entry utilizes an anchored buoy connected with a taut visible line. Swim up to the line and commence your surface dive. Try to follow the vertical line straight down.

Your return to the surface should appear almost effortless. As you ascend past your neutral point, slow your kicking stroke. Stop kicking approximately 5 feet (1.5 meters) below the surface. About 6 to 10 inches (15 to 25 centimeters) below the surface, clear the snorkel of water by releasing breath into your snorkel.

Further into the surface dive, after you have cleared your ears, you'll need to equalize the pressure on your mask.

Exercise 15: Mask equalization. Release your ear-clearing finger pressure from under the nose pocket and blow a small amount of air from your nose into the mask—just enough to maintain comfort but not so much that you make air bubbles.

To show how excessive mask pressure distorts vision, try this exercise. Swim to the bottom of a 10-foot (3-meter) to 12-foot (4-meter) pool. On the way down, make no attempt to equalize the pressure building up on your faceplate. On the bottom, focus on an object and then release air into the mask. Notice how the apparent distance to the object changes.

Beyond the surface dive

Exercise 16: Hula-hoop swim. Once you have mastered the three fin kicks, ear equalization, and the surface dive, combine them in a underwater obstacle course. Place a series of weighted and anchored hula hoops at different depths throughout the pool. Swim through these hoops as if you were mimicking a sea lion. Try swimming face down, sideways and face up. This is an excellent exercise to develop directional control and position sense underwater.

Exercise 17: Your base underwater

Exercise 16: Hula-hoop swim

At this point, it's time to learn another relaxation awareness-building exercise. This exercise will assist your efforts to separate a hyper-alert mind from a dormant body. As with all pool exercises, make sure you have an observer ready to assist you in the event you over-extend your dive.

Exercise 17: Establishing your base underwater. Swim to the bottom of the pool. Lie at ease by summoning the feeling you learned in the relaxed fetal position exercise. Shut your eyes, forget your limp body and concentrate on sounds in the pool— noise from the pool motor or the sound your instructor makes when he scratches the side of the pool. Repeat this exercise with your eyes open. Start with an expanded view of the pool bottom and then narrow your focus to a dime or a tiny imperfection on the bottom.

ADVANCED FREEDIVING EXERCISES

Moving underwater

Freedivers move slowly and effortlessly through the water. Because our air supply is limited, we strive for efficiency—every action must have a reason, otherwise it's a waste of precious energy. Our goal is to cover greatest area with the least amount of effort. Become conscious of your "projecting drag area," be as streamlined as possible and optimize your fins' action by using proper technique. Increasing your speed won't help. In general, doubling your speed underwater quadruples your energy consumption.

Exercise 18: The ruler exercise. The ruler exercise helps demonstrate the importance of a streamlined profile. Take an ordinary ruler and hold it in front of you lengthwise just below the surface. Start swimming and face the broad end of the ruler into your path. The ruler adds considerable drag to your profile and slows you. If this small ruler has such a pronounced effect, you can imagine the drag created by your chest or other parts of your body when your diving form is not streamlined. Now, tip the ruler on its edge and you'll

National Freediving Champion Gerald Lim demonstrates an excellent streamlined position.

Gerald mimics an overweighted diver. Note how he deflects water off the front of his chest and creates eddy-currents behind him.

Gerald demonstrates streamlining problems of the underweighted diver as he struggles to get deeper.

notice a significant reduction in drag as well as a corresponding increase in your speed.

When water washes over your streamlined body in a smooth, laminar flow, you can move more efficiently with less exertion and hold your breath longer. Align your body so that it is perfectly parallel to your direction of travel. In this position, water flows around your body with no abrupt changes of direction. When water strikes anything projecting from your body, it quickly changes course. Water will actually reverse its direction and make small eddy currents that cause a parachute-like effect behind you.

What causes this excessive drag? Improper weighting is one cause. An over-weighted diver swims diagonally through the water instead of horizontally.

The extra weight causes his legs and fins to drag downward as he kicks forward and upward in an attempt to compensate for the weight. Under-weighted divers also swim diagonally but in reverse. In an attempt to move forward, kicking drives their head and shoulders downward while their legs and fins lift.

Avoid using your hands to assist with underwater swimming because they're a major source of drag. Keep them in front of you or along your side. Try streamlining your flutter kick by narrowing the distance between each leg stroke and increasing the number of cycles. Don't over exaggerate your fin stroke. "Overkicking" causes your fins and legs to break through your body's smooth horizontal plane and creates eddies and drag.

Exercise 18: The ruler exercise

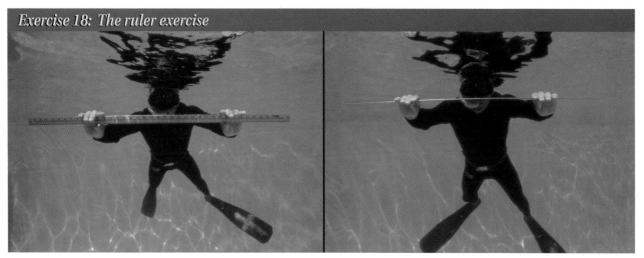

During the vertical portions of your dive, your head and shoulders are potential sources of drag. On descent, completely invert your head while keeping your arms either outstretched in front (Superman posture) or folded at your groin. Placing your hands along your side "squares up" your shoulders and causes massive drag, particularly when you ascend. Test the difference yourself: ascend with your hands placed along your side, and then try it with your hands folded in your groin. (Pinching your right thumb between your left pointing finger and thumb seems to help.) In the last position, notice that your shoulders are slightly rounded and that you have no muscular tension in your neck and shoulders. You should ascend faster without additional effort.

Increasing your vital capacity

One factor that determines how long you can hold your breath is the vital capacity of your lungs—the total amount of air that is moved during a maximum inhalation and exhalation. You can increase your vital capacity through training and constant freediving. Practicing deep, slow resistance breathing should help increase your vital capacity. Try breathing through a small-diameter hose or tube or blowing up balloons.

"Packing" is another technique designed to increase vital capacity. Many divers have independently rediscovered this technique. Both David and National Champion John Ernst feel that this exercise promotes healthy chest compliance and makes the first dive of the day as good as the last. It was a common technique used by the United States Naval Submariner Trainers in Groton, Connecticut, as well as Navy Seal divers. Deep freediver Bob Croft may have been the originator of this technique.

To pack your lungs, you gulp air. After a deep inhalation to capacity, you force more air into your lungs by using your cheek and throat muscles to push the air in. Physiologist Bill Hamilton found that test subjects who used this packing technique could increase their vital capacity by 1.2 to 1.7 liters.

Packing may cause your chest to feel full and tight, like it's going to burst—a feeing that quickly dissipates after you descend a few feet. Some feel that the effort required by this technique negates its advantages. Others disagree. It should be noted that this technique is not without risk. In susceptible individuals, pressure in the lungs theoretically might rise enough to cause a rupture of the lung's delicate lining, which then could lead to an air embolism.

Increasing tolerance to apneic conditions

"Apnea" is the term divers and physiologists use to describe the condition of breath holding. There must be as many methods to increase breath-holding times as there are divers in the world. Their common goal is to develop a tolerance to the consequences of breath holding—carbon dioxide excess and oxygen deficits. Below, we summarize just a few training tips from divers around the country. While we do not endorse or condone any of these techniques, we list them in an effort to describe what others do. Always evaluate an exercise from the point of view of safety, with the advice of your instructor, and have a spotter standing by for assistance. Remember that prolonged breath-hold diving can be dangerous causing unconsciousness and subsequent drowning.

Exercise 19: Apnea walk. Lay out a course on land in 25-foot (7.5-meter), 50-foot (15-meter), 75-foot (23-meter) and 100-foot (30-meter) lengths. Take your usual three to four deep breaths in preparation for a dive, hold your breath and then walk to the end of the various distances and return. Practice doing something, like taking a picture at each distance before returning. Besides building physical tolerance, this exercise offers some confidence to the diver who can now visualize the distance he must travel underwater.

Exercise 20: Apnea push ups. This exercise helps you build further tolerance to high carbon dioxide levels and oxygen debt on land. Lie on your back and breathe slowly. Take your last breath and hold it for a minute. When the minute is up, continue to hold your breath, roll over and perform as many push ups as possible.

Exercise 21: Underwater pushes. To increase both your breath-hold time and your balance underwater, dive to the bottom of the pool and, while keeping your

Exercise 21: Underwater pushes

body vertical with your hands down, simply push against it. Make sure that you have a spotter whenever you exert yourself underwater.

Exercise 22: U.R.I. breathing exercise. David learned this exercise, dubbed the "University of Rhode Island breathing exercise," when he taught scientific diving at the University of Rhode Island. Walt Hendricks, Sr., former Training Director of the National Association of Underwater Instructors (NAUI), is credited with developing this exercise, which invokes the bradycardia reflex and increases breath-hold times.

Exercise 22: U.R.I. Breathing exercise

For this group exercise, you'll need three or more divers and a timer/spotter at pool side. Be sure to practice the exercise as described—no short cuts. Wearing no gear other than swimwear, form a circle in water waist deep. Inhale and exhale slowly, keeping the exhalation phase twice as long as the inhalation phase. The only participant allowed to talk or use a mask is the timer/spotter.

When everyone is relaxed and using the same breathing cycle, gently hold hands and float face down into the water. You may either sink or float as you relax into the now-familiar feeling of the floating fetal position. Hold your breath for ten seconds. Keep holding hands until the timer says, "Time's up." Hand holding serves several purposes: it keeps students from drifting away; it serves as a means of communication and it's a good measure of individual tension.

When you surface, remain calm and relaxed while you breathe deeply for one minute. Now, submerge again and increase your breath-hold time to 20 seconds. Back at the surface, breathe slowly and deeply for another minute. Submerge once more, this time for 30 seconds. On the surface, resume another one-minute surface interval. Continue to increase your breath-holding times in 15-second increments, and increase the surface period to a minute-and-a-half to two minutes between dives. Repeat the exercise until you achieve two minutes underwater—an excellent stopping point. Some divers, after a month's practice, repeating this exercise two to three times per week, reach breath-hold times of two to four minutes!

Exercise 23: Dolphin breaching. This exercise is excellent for those interested in underwater hockey or who make shallow, fast, repetitive dives. By mimicking marine mammals that exhale and inhale at the surface in mid-stroke without stopping, this exercise emphasizes breathing, speed and efficiency. You'll need your mask, snorkel and fins. Besides teaching pacing, this exercise rather quickly extends your confidence and apnea ability.

Relaxed, slowly swim underwater one-half the length of the pool. Surface just long enough for a breath then swim the remaining half of the pool. Continue the drill by swimming underwater with just three breaks for air—one at each end of the pool and one in the middle. If you swim too fast, are tense or cold, you'll need more than one breath. If you're too slow, you might not be able to reach the designated breathing spots. Repeat the exercise for 15 minutes, until you're tired or you develop a "carbon dioxide headache."

GRADUATING TO THE OPEN WATER

Remember our honeymooners? Imagine how the young lady would have benefited from competent instruction and pool training. Yet, there are two remaining obstacles any diver needs to overcome before succeeding as a confident, competent and relaxed open-water diver: gaining familiarity and confidence in one's gear and coping with a new environment and "fear of the unknown."

Besides the basic gear you've already mastered, there is one more item that you should test in the pool before you take it to the open water: your wetsuit. For physiological reasons, an ill-fitting wetsuit can quickly increase your apprehension levels and destroy your first open-water experience.

Try your wetsuit for short periods in the pool and test your performance by repeating some basic exercises. If you feel uncomfortable, check the fit of your wetsuit in two critical areas: around your neck and around your chest. A wetsuit that's too tight at the neck can impinge on the major arteries of your head and neck and cause considerable distress and possible blackout. Symptoms might include light-headedness, or more frequently, claustrophobia. If you experience either, have a professional suitmaker loosen the neck. Check the tightness of the rubber over your chest. If your suit is too tight, it will prevent the full expansion of your chest and make deep breathing difficult. Don't be discouraged if initially your performance decreases while wearing a wetsuit—that's normal and in time you'll become accustomed to it.

After you're comfortable with your wetsuit, you're finished with your basic pool training. The last hurdle, fear of the unknown, can't be managed in the pool. Initially, everyone worries about what's going to eat their dangling extremities. Poor water conditions—diminished visibility, choppy seas and currents—magnify the worry. For your first open-water experience, your instructor should choose a suitable transition location such as a calm, clear, shallow bay.

Repeat all the pool exercises in the open water, starting with the relaxed fetal position. Repeat mask and fin exercises. Check for vertical descent. Dive to the bottom and repeat the concentration exercises that heighten mental awareness while the rest of your body sleeps. By now, your confidence level should be high enough for you to begin exploring your world underwater, out on the reefs or in the bluewater. Rather quickly, you'll make the transition from instruction-based dives to dives you plan yourself. If you have not already joined a club, this is an excellent time to locate a club or group of divers interested in freediving. The Underwater Society of America has lists of member freediving clubs in your area.

Exercise 24: The fish test for smoothness. For this exercise, you'll need to locate a school of fish. When you can swim among and through a school of fish without disturbing them, your body form and kicking stroke are optimum.

USING YOUR SENSES UNDERWATER

Your five terrestrial senses are all altered underwater. Your sense of taste and smell disappear, and your gloved body attenuates the sense of touch. Sound travels four times faster underwater, so fast that you can't tell from which direction a sound emanated. Nevertheless, learn to tune into underwater sounds; they'll tell you a great deal about your surroundings—whales sing, dolphins whistle and

Gerald Lim demonstrates exercise 24, the fish test for smoothness.
When you can swim among and through a school of fish without disturbing
them, your body form and kicking stroke are optimum.

click, some fish grunt or croak and shrimp click and pop. Sometimes you can hear the shore break tumbling rocks in the waves.

Your most reliable sense underwater is sight. Even this sense is restricted by your mask, water visibility and anxiety level. While beginning freedivers "look" into the water, trained divers "see." Novice divers are often unaware of what's around them because they are trying to look at everything as quickly as possible rather than taking a slow, methodical approach. It's not uncommon for beginning divers to swim over

marine life without a clue of its presence.

Look for contrasting objects, textures or colors. Anything moving is likely to attract your attention. Remember to look in all directions, side to side, up and down and even behind you. Move your head slowly, pausing frequently to look out and beyond, and then focus on something close. Don't always expect a large, panoramic view. On poor-visibility days, your world underwater will contract to a few feet in diameter. Even these days can be rewarding. Your short focus often reveals enough of the bottom to make a dive exciting.

ROUGH SURF ENTRIES

This section should help you prepare for rough-surf entries and exits. Although there is no single method that works well in all surf conditions, we'll suggest some general techniques.

Before you enter the water, you need to "read" the waves and the surf sets. Waves most often arrive in groups that are repetitive and therefore predictable. Gauge the height of the breaking waves—the higher the wave, the greater amount of energy released when the wave breaks. Learn to respect this awesome power. Next, look for a sandy area. In rough surf, avoid rocky areas because of the potential for serious injury that exists if you are thrown against or over sharp rocks.

Just before you enter the water, make sure all equipment is in place. To help secure your fins, use fixie poms, modified over-boots or duct-tape. There is a cardinal rule that you must not break: never turn your back on the sea. Since you'll want to walk backward into the surf to prevent losing your fins, you'll have to turn your head to keep an eye on the surf.

Wait for the wave set with the smallest waves. Once you're committed to "go," do not stop swimming until you have passed the surf zone. Swim with one arm stretched out in front of you because foam and bubbles may obscure what's in front. Keep your other hand on your mask. If a wave is going to break on you, dive to within a foot or two of the bottom. Be sure your body is stretched out and perpendicular to the wave.

When you enter the surf, there is a cardinal rule that you must not break: never turn your back on the sea.

Tow your float behind you. Never attempt to push it because the wave might carry it back to the beach with you attached or throw the float into you. Most important, do not delay in "no man's land"—the surf zone—since it's easy to become exhausted and disoriented there. Expect to use an enormous amount of energy when you traverse the surf zone. Try to pace yourself, but get through the surf as quickly as possible.

Exiting is similar to entering: timing is very important. Wait outside the surf zone and read the sets. Swimming as quickly as you can, follow the first small set to shore. Be prepared for the "backwash" of some waves as they travel backward. You may find it necessary to hold on to the bottom and kick vigorously just to hold your ground. Don't be alarmed if you lose ground—it often happens. Let the next wave push you forward. On the beach, keep all gear in place as you crawl on your hands and knees out of the water. Be sure to clear the water before you remove any gear. Remember, you just exited on the small wave set; larger waves with more force may arrive at any moment to sweep your precious equipment away.

A word of caution: never tie anything to yourself or you may become entangled with your gear, the bottom or your buddy.

FREEDIVING ACCIDENTS

Freediving accidents are relatively rare. You can prevent most of them by obtaining professional instruction and using forethought and common sense. Please refer to the physiology chapters for a review of hypoxia, hypothermia, stress and panic. Below, we'll summarize the other common causes of dive accidents. Again, this discussion is not a substitute for proper professional training, but rather a supplement to your professional training program. Because of Murphy's Law—sooner or later, anything that can go wrong will go wrong—we firmly believe freedivers should study first aid and CPR.

Line tangles

Because of your limited supply of air, anything that impedes your return to the surface is dangerous. It's possible to become entangled with fish nets, buoy lines, almost-invisible monofilament fishing line and your own float line. Carry a sharp knife and be

When you see sharks, it's best to move to another location.

prepared to use it. Make sure you can reach it with either hand and practice removing it from its sheath. We've seen situations when divers thought that they could reach their knife but because of its position they could not. Dive cautiously near lines and nets, especially when the visibility is poor. Move slowly and monitor the water in front of you.

Marine life

Coral scrapes and abrasions cause the majority of injuries suffered by freedivers. Most other marine injuries stem from the defensive reactions of the offended animal. Make a study of marine life in your area by consulting local fish guides and by discussing potential problems with your local dive shop. Stings from jelly fish and fire coral are painful. Be sure to watch where you swim, especially when you approach the surface, and wear protective garments such as a dive skin. For effective protection against mats of

Portuguese man-of-war jellyfish, the South Africans slip panty hose over their face and cut holes for their eyes and mouth. As a general rule, if you can't identify an organism, don't touch it.

Novice freedivers often fear kelp forests, believing that the thick mats of weed will entangle them. In reality, most of the plant they see is floating on the surface. Below the surface, there is ample room for the freediver to maneuver. Getting through the surface mat is likewise quite easy. Before you dive, clear a small area for your surface entry with your hands. When you ascend, look for a break in the kelp. If the kelp mat is solid, raise one arm straight above you. When you surface, let your hand pierce the seaweed mat and sweep away an area for your head and snorkel. It's actually quite easy to dive in the kelp forest, and because of its three dimensions and prolific marine life, quite exciting.

Sharks! Just the word is enough to keep potential freedivers from enjoying the sport. Except for the rare great white shark, most sharks give ample warning of their presence. When you see a shark, react calmly and move to another dive spot. Many spearfishers, especially bluewater divers, routinely swim with the sharks. These divers constantly monitor the sharks' behavior and move at the first sign of aggressiveness. Most times a gentle prod with a sharp rod or speargun is enough to discourage the most curious shark.

Physical conditioning and fatigue

Many diving accidents result from exhaustion and poor physical conditioning. Stay in shape, dive only when you feel well and stay within your personal limits. If you are diving in a group, consider the ability of the least experienced diver as a guideline to plan the length and scope of your dive session. Don't be embarrassed if you feel that the conditions exceed your limits, and never force a reluctant buddy to dive. If you feel fatigued, rest for a while or quit for the day. If possible, avoid untested medications and never use any intoxicating liquors or drugs.

Boat encounters

Boat traffic is a major concern for freedivers because of our limited time underwater. Once you begin your ascent, you typically have to surface immediately. Our advice is to save some reserve time for your ascent and use discretion in choosing a dive site. Avoid diving in heavy boat traffic, near personal watercraft or in other confined, multi-use areas. Not only do boaters have rights to the same waters, but many are simply not aware of the possibility of freedivers sharing the same space. Be sure to fly the appropriate divers-down flag and don't assume that all people know what the flag means.

Equipment malfunctions

The beauty of freediving is that our equipment is simple and durable, and it's not prone to malfunction. Nonetheless, you should anticipate gear problems— masks can flood, fins and weight belts can fall off and some fins may even break. Be prepared to deal with each event by practicing in the pool. Remember, if you think you might be low on air, drop your weight belt. Always use complete, well-maintained equipment.

Your dive buddy

Dive with a buddy whenever possible. There is always safety in numbers, and most divers enjoy sharing their experiences with others. Even if your buddy is unable to assist you, at least that person knows your general location. If you do dive alone, be sure to leave your detailed dive plan with a friend and notify that person if your plan changes.

We hope we have made our message clear: freediving, like most sports, depends on professional training, good gear and liberal doses of common sense. Had the honeymooner, mentioned earlier, been properly introduced to her gear and received advance pool training, her Hawaiian experience would have been pleasurable instead of disappointing. Safety in the water requires forethought. You should have a plan to handle common emergencies, and you should pause a few seconds to consider what might go wrong before you attempt something new. Freediving takes commitment. Make that commitment and you'll enjoy an exciting, rewarding sport for your entire life.

There is no finer freediving asset than your dive buddy.

This image of a freediver earned professional photographer
Jeff Rotman the coveted National Press Photographers award.

Freediving photography

Freediving offers a multitude of opportunities for capturing magnificent underwater images of shy, elusive subjects. Whether it's with a still camera or a video recorder, silent, graceful freedivers often produce pictures others miss. Many world-class underwater photographers have set aside their scuba gear in search of better pictures. A short list includes such greats as Bill Boyce, Al Giddings, Howard Hall, Chuck and Flip Nicklin, Doug Perrine, Rick Rosenthal, Brian Skerry, James D. Watt and Norbert Wu.

In this chapter, we'll cover the basics of film and video photography with generous contributions from California freediving photographers Harrison A. "Skip" Stubbs, Ph.D., and Phil Colla. Both men, with their natural swimming abilities and photographic experience, evolved from occasional scuba photographers into passionate, top-notch, large-animal image-makers—from amateur to professional in just about five years by freediving.

This chapter offers a simplified approach to underwater photography. Readers interested in learning more about this subject should read Howard Hall's *Guide to Successful Underwater Photography* (last published by Macor Publishing, 1990) or the *Pisces Guide to Shooting Underwater Video* by Steve Rosenberg and John Ratterree (Gulf Publishing Co., 1991).

PRINCIPLES COMMON TO VIDEO AND STILL PHOTOGRAPHY

The distance between you and your subject is important for two reasons: focus and color filtration. Fish are generally far enough from the lens (more than 5 to 7 feet or 1.5 to 2 meters) that problems with focusing, common with macro (close) shots, are minimal. With the appropriate film selection, f-stop and shutter speed, it should be easy to preset the lens focus for a range of 5 to 12 feet (1.5 to 3.5 meters). For large, distant, marine animals, keep the infinity setting within your camera's depth-of-field.

Color filtration increases with the length of the water column through which light travels. Include in your calculations both the distance between you and your subject and the distance from the subject to the surface. Warm colors, first the reds and next the yellows, are absorbed so quickly that most images shot through a color-absorbing water column of more than 15 feet (4.5 meters), are condemned to shades of blue. The light-absorbing property of water is the same for a subject 1 foot away (36 centimeters) and 14 feet (4.2 meters) below the water as it is for a subject 14 feet away and 1 foot under the water.

Hawaiian spinner dolphins. The most colorful images are made on sunny days in shallow water with the subject next to the lens.

The most colorful images are made on sunny days in shallow water with the subject next to the lens. Wide-angle lenses allow you to get close enough for quality color, yet they don't cut off parts of your subject, like narrower angled lenses do. By brushing water across the lens surface with your hand, you can remove small air bubbles that collect, especially just after entering the water or encountering foamy surface water. Don't touch the lens—you might leave streaks. Amber color-correction filters, by selectively blocking the blues, help restore color to pictures shot through a long water column.

Professional photographers typically avoid the use of these filters, preferring instead to correct their images in the lab. One disadvantage of these filters is that they decrease light, thus requiring the lens to open wider. This results in less depth-of-field (the range of distance that subjects will be in sharp focus). A parallel disadvantage of using filters with still cameras is that the resulting decreased light requires a slower shutter speed if you choose to keep the lens opening unchanged. Loss of light is rarely a big problem with subjects that do not move—sea fans, for example—since you can simply adjust the shutter speed down a few notches. With bluewater species that typically move quickly, this is not an option. So you're faced with a dilemma: little depth-of-field or slow shutter speed?

However, filters are useful in newer video housings, equipped with flip-down filters and large color monitors, making it possible for on-the-spot color correction.

For subjects closer than 6 feet (2 meters), strobes are useful to add color to a deep-water subject or to subtly wash a surface image with color-enhancing light. Bluewater creatures like tuna are often highly reflective, so much so that they light up like mirrors when shot with strobes. To subdue the strobe's effect, try a strobe-diffuser or a lower power setting. On the other hand, many bluewater animals (bottlenose dolphin, mola-mola) have muted colors which look unnatural and usually displeasing when lit with artificial light. Phil Colla suggests you shoot shy or rare animals first without strobes. After you have secured a few satisfactory images, you might risk scaring the animal with artificial light or by introducing strobe-induced artifacts into the environment.

VIDEO RECORDING

According to Rick Rosenthal, video recorders offer several advantages over film cameras: they're less expensive and quieter than noisy film cameras—you can get closer to shy subjects. Another advantage of video recorders is their "low-lux" capability—the ability to capture images in very low-light situations. There is a price to pay, however; as the light decreases, expect images to become more grainy and monochromatic. Finally, of course, video cameras can record sound, which is of great value to those wishing to document the raucous clicking of rock shrimp or the serenades of singing whales.

In just a few years, Skip Stubbs has become a freediving convert from scuba and a master underwater videographer. In 1961, Skip earned an informal scuba certification. Although he is a strong swimmer and enjoys the feeling of being underwater, the cold he experienced from inadequate wetsuits and his studies in biostatistics kept him an occasional diver until years later. In 1985, Skip recertified in scuba and began his diving avocation in earnest.

"It was not until I dove Guadalupe Island, Mexico, in 1991, that I started to appreciate the advantages of freediving," he recalls. "We were suiting up over open water when someone noticed oceanic white-tip sharks circling nearby. Fearing I'd miss the photo opportunity, I skipped my scuba gear and grabbed my mask, snorkel and camera. I was able to stay with the sharks for nearly two hours, and I realized that my success was due solely to my freediving approach."

Over the next few years, Skip's interests turned to larger, more intelligent marine animals—seals, dolphins and whales. "The bigger the animal I saw, the bigger I wanted to see," he says. "I really enjoy marine mammals when they approach, turning toward me—clearly displaying their intelligence and curiosity. Those instances where I have been able to establish acceptance through my actions and demeanor have been the most rewarding, both

PHOTO: BRIAN SKERRY

A Florida manatee.

93

Skip Stubbs films a sunfish off Southern California.

personally and in terms of capturing images."

In 1993, Skip's interest in marine mammals shifted to whales. He joined Dr. Dan Salden and the Hawaii Whale Research Foundation as a research associate to help teach fellow researchers the use of underwater video equipment. What was planned as a 10-day trip evolved into a four-week adventure with remarkable whale encounters.

"It's a very special experience when a whale comes close enough to you to get interested and rolls its 45-ton body to eye you," Skip says. "I don't know anybody who has looked a whale in the eye and watched its focus shift toward them who has not been profoundly affected by the encounter."

Skip is intrigued with the whale's occasional, almost-human curiosity. Before his personal encounters with these large animals, Skip thought that whales would be unaware of him. He's since learned that, although they usually ignore him, they always know he's present.

Through his work as a research scientist with Dr. Salden's group, Skip has developed his personal view toward marine mammals. "I consider myself a guest in their presence and behave accordingly," he says. "I just want to be a passive observer. I'm interested in capturing normal behavior in a natural environment, not creating a situation where the animals are affected by my presence. I prefer them to be neither repelled nor attracted—just accepting."

Many of Skip's sentiments are reflected in two federal laws: the Marine Mammal Protection Act and the Endangered Species Act. With specific reference to the humpback whales in Hawaii, the laws prohibit any behavior that harasses or otherwise adversely affects whale behavior or creates situations where the mammals must alter their behavior to avoid contact with you. You are prohibited from approaching within 100 yards (90 meters) of humpbacks, and may not "leapfrog" into their path, either on your boat or swimming. You need particularly to be aware that

94

Skip films two graceful creatures.

approaching endangered species such as the North Pacific humpback whale in United States waters is prohibited without proper research or photographic permits (available from the National Marine Fisheries Service). Furthermore, while the appropriate regulations restrict your approach to these species, the laws do not prohibit them from approaching you; it is still your burden, however, to prove that they initiated the approach.

While the humpback whales wintering in Hawaii are protected from other-than-chance human contact (unless you have a research permit), there are other locations in the world where freedivers may approach whales: Atlantic humpbacks at the Silver Banks off the Turks and Caicos Islands; South Pacific humpbacks off Tonga; sperm whales off the Azores and minke whales off Australia. Except for the calving lagoons of Baja California, Mexico, you may generally approach gray whales anywhere, provided you do so in a cautious, non-harassing manner.

Skip agrees with us that the best video images are taken in water no deeper than 35 feet (10.5 meters). Under ideal conditions, when there is full sunlight shining straight down into very clear water, this depth can extend to 50 feet (15 meters). Try to aim horizontally or upward, and keep the sun at your back. For crisp images use shutter speeds of 1/125 to 1/250 in shallow, clear water. When the water is dirty or deep, or the sun is behind clouds or at a low angle, place the shutter-speed setting on "auto" (1/60 second).

Let's examine the equipment. The most popular video recorders for underwater image-making use the small, clear Hi-8 format or the newer digital (DV) format. Manufacturers are constantly improving video cameras and their housings. Skip currently uses a three-chip Panasonic digital camera in a Video-Sea housing. A comparable system is the Sony series of video recorders. They operate for an average of two hours using a single battery. An improved auto-focus feature decreases "hunting," which is the transient

Freediving offers photographers the best opportunity to capture shy hammerhead sharks on film. On the previous page, researchers document the behavior of the humpback whale. Both photos are by Phil Colla.

in-and-out lens motion of the electronic circuitry focusing on an image. The Sony's modest size permits a small housing, which leads to increased maneuverability.

One of the finest consumer video housings is the Stingray, manufactured by Light and Motion Industries. Its small size, superior optics, electronic controls, expertly crafted seals and locking mechanisms make this a versatile and reliable housing for the bluewater hunter. With just three housing penetrations—one for the backplate, one for the lens and one for the flip-down color filter—the number of possible water leakage points is minimal. Compared to most other housings, camera installation is simple. All cable connections are made from the camera to a docking plate outside the housing, where big fingers are no problem. The whole assembly is inserted into the housing, which

The Stingray video housing manufactured by Light and Motion Industries.

PHOTO: TERRY MAAS

Spinner dolphin families cruise the shallow waters off Hawaii.

receives the electronic connections from the docking plate, much like plugging in an electrical outlet. For purposes of illustration, we'll highlight each aspect of video recording and relate it to a specific feature available on the Stingray.

Focusing is easy for the photographer unconcerned with close-up images. The 90-degree, optically correct lens is unique among other housings because of its ability to maintain focus throughout the full zoom range. For fixed-distance subjects, set the focus once and zoom away. (Fixing the focus at 5 to 10 feet—1.5 to 4.5 meters—provides sufficient depth-of-field in most instances.)

Should you use the auto-focus feature of the video recorder? The answer depends on light conditions, the subject and your experience with the camera. We prefer to use the auto-focus mode to "snap to focus" on the subject and, once focused, we disable the auto-focus, leaving the camera fix-focused in the manual mode. Leaving the recorder set in the auto-focus mode risks the possibility of the electronic circuitry temporarily losing focus and

"hunting" as it adjusts in and out in an attempt to recapture the correct focus. The resulting image is blurry and ruins the sequence. Auto-focus circuitry becomes more dependable in highly illuminated, clean water and less reliable in poorly illuminated, dirty water.

Use the Stingray's 3-inch color monitor to accurately compose your shot, monitor color reproduction (white balance) and check the displayed camera functions. View the monitor with the recorder held relaxed in front of your chest, instead of close up against your eye. The advantage of arms-length viewing is that you can see your target easily, over the camera, thus simplifying adjustments to your aim. Do not use it for focus, as your eye cannot accurately judge fine-focus through the monitor.

White balance is the setting responsible for the correct representation of color. It's usually set at "sunlight" or "auto," but you can experiment with the proper setting while shooting. Professionals set white balance with a white slate they carry; viewing the slate for five seconds through the lens establishes

99

PHOTO: TERRY MAAS

Sherry Shaffer glides with a manta ray over a submerged pinnacle.

the best balance. It's also possible to adjust color balance later in the lab with professional post-production editing electronics.

Another way to adjust the camera for the light-filtering effects of water is to use the Stingray's flip-down color-correction filter hinged inside the camera housing. Use it to restore red and yellow colors when shooting through a water column more than 15 feet (4.5 meters) long. The filter is most effective when light is plentiful—for example, clear tropical waters between the hours of 10 a.m. and 3 p.m. The filter will help to restore warm colors in both a turbid water column of up to 20 feet (6 meters) and a clean water column of up to 50 feet (15 meters). Check the filter's effect in the monitor; it may introduce a red tint to the image, especially near the surface or pointing toward the sun.

STILL PHOTOGRAPHY

Whether they're filming whales for research or sunfish for fun, Skip Stubbs and Phil Colla often work as a team: Skip uses his video recorder and Phil uses his still camera. Many of the images in this chapter and in the companion video to this book, *The Joy of Freediving*, were taken by these men.

Phil Colla has always lived near the ocean. In high school, Phil learned surfing and still photography. In 1988, after college, Phil tried scuba diving and found that he was a natural at the sport. After four to five years, when the novelty of the sport waned, he took his first underwater photographs. He credits his early success to his previous knowledge of photography and lighting.

In 1991, Phil met his mentor, Skip Stubbs, who soon helped Phil realize that he really hadn't seen much in his underwater forays. They became friends. Phil observed that Skip looked for opportunities to film however they came. He learned, too, that freediving actually increased his underwater photo opportunities. Eventually, Phil began freediving more as his focus shifted to images of large marine mammals. He noticed that many of his best shots were made while freediving.

Since 1994, when Skip introduced him to cetaceans and Dr. Dan Salden, Phil has assisted the Hawaii Whale Research Foundation as a volunteer research associate. Today, Phil takes most of his images while freediving. "Quick entry into the water and freedom of movement are real assets,"

PHOTO: TERRY MAAS

*Don't overlook the powerful
impact of a silhouette image.*

PHOTO: JEFF ROTMAN

The Nikonos-V is the camera of choice of many amateurs and professionals.

he says. "Since most of our subjects are air-breathers living near the surface, I find that I can approach these animals in a non-threatening manner by freediving. Swimming into the blue without tanks simply feels great!"

Phil cautions against trying to master underwater photography and freediving at the same time. He recommends that you obtain a solid grounding in either discipline before attempting to combine them.

Phil considers the Nikonos-V camera the best choice for freedivers because it's small, light and versatile. Its ease of operation decreases the confusion in exciting situations. You can even use this camera "shooting from the hip." Phil knows of a diver who holds his camera at arms length for dolphin photos and manages to center 80 percent of his images without the viewfinder. The trick is to mark an "X" (diagonally from corner to corner) on the back of the backplate to locate the center of the camera. Simply aim the "X" at your subject and shoot.

A disadvantage of the Nikonos-V is that the camera does not feature through-the-lens viewing, or focusing. It's up to you to estimate distances underwater—something you must master with practice. Remember, if an object appears to be 6 feet (1.8 meters) away it's really 7-1/2 feet (2.3 meters) away—25 percent farther.

While the 35-millimeter amphibious lens that comes with the camera is good for long shots—typically greater than 10 feet (3 meters), the length of the water column washes out most of the color. Using a wider angle lens lets you get much closer to your subject, decreasing the water column and increasing

color and contrast. The wide-angle 28-millimeter, 20-millimeter and 15-millimeter lenses work well and are all optically corrected for exclusive underwater use. The 15-millimeter lens, with 94 degrees of coverage, allows you to shoot within the closest range—1 to 3 feet (.03 to 1 meter) in natural light and 6 inches (15 centimeters) with strobes—but this lens is expensive ($800 to $1,500). This is the lens of choice for portraits of divers and wrecks.

The more reasonable 28-millimeter lens, with its 59-degree angle of coverage and a minimum focus of two feet (0.7 meters), costs about $300. This lens is ideal for beginners who like to shoot fish portraits. It can do everything the 35-millimeter lens can with higher quality. Prefocus, set the depth-of-field and leave it alone.

The Nikonos 20-millimeter lens is the best all-purpose wide-angle lens available, especially considering that it is roughly half the price of the 15-millimeter lens—about $800. The 20-millimeter is optically sharp, rivaling the 15-millimeter lens when you focus it properly. This lens has a narrower field-of-view than the 15-millimeter, which is advantageous when shooting timid animals that keep their distance. You can fill the frame with your subject more easily with the 20-millimeter. When focused at a distance of 3 feet (1 meter) and beyond, this lens has a generous depth-of-field. Because this lens is smaller than the bulky 15-millimeter, it's less likely to become jarred loose, which can cause the camera to flood. "The 20-millimeter lens has to be the most versatile of the Nikonos lenses," says Phil. "It's my personal favorite."

The majority of the best images, dependent on natural light, are made on calm, sunny days, between 10 a.m. and 2 p.m., by aiming upward at a slight angle toward the surface. This offers a beautifully variegated background, dramatic perspective and the chance for enhancing rays of light to stream through the image. Be careful in overcast skies, though. When you point upward in such situations, the surface in the background of the picture becomes washed out and ugly and may, for some films, bleed into the subject area. When it's overcast, try to shoot level or slightly downward.

Look for composition; a small fish in the frame enhances the quality of the image by adding perspective, both in size and distance. (See the image of Sherry Shaffer on the next page.) For spearfishers, don't forget the trick of making a speared fish appear bigger by positioning it closer to the lens than its captor.

To beginning freediving photographers, experts suggest the following guidelines: for level or upward

Sherry and the manta ray.

PHOTO: BOB CARUSO

shots, shoot at a speed of 1/60-second. Shoot at 1/30-second when pointing down. Use 100 ASA film or faster. Film selection is based on experience. James Watt suggests using Kodachrome 64 for water that is more blue than green, and Fujichrome Provia for water more green than blue. In low-light conditions, without a flash, try Kodak's Ektachrome E100SW, ASA 100 (professional grade), setting the ASA to 200 on the camera. Be sure to tell the developer to "push" the film one stop.

All of the films mentioned produce slide transparencies, which are preferred by professionals who project their work or expect to sell it to magazines. Beginners who want snapshots for their friends might consider using print film, which offers greater latitude in colors and exposure settings. One problem with print films, however, is that "one-hour labs" create their prints by machine based on settings for skin tones and other above-water characteristics. This often leads to water colors that are washed out or simply incorrect. You may need to return the negatives to the lab requesting printing for more pleasing, realistic colors.

Since water is a little darker than 18% gray, the target for average slide film, you may need to "underexpose" scenes that contain a large component of blue water. To compensate, decrease the iris opening (for example, change f/8 to f/8.5) or adjust the shutter speed (for example, shoot at 1/90-second instead of 1/60-second).

"While strobes do restore colors to subjects deeper than 15 feet (4.5 meters), they greatly complicate the photography process," advises Phil. "I prefer to shoot in water 15 to 30 feet (4.5 to 9 meters) deep and wait for animals to come to me. When I get an opportunity to film a new animal, I shoot a half roll of film without the strobes to guarantee the basic image. I remember shooting an elusive Galapagos fur seal when I captured excellent natural-light images. All of my strobe shots were substandard, complicated with such strobe-induced artifacts as back scatter and unnaturally bright, white eyes. Had I started with the strobe, I might have missed all of my shots!"

We suggest that you hold your strobe in one hand and your camera in the other. Separate the two by several feet. Keeping the source of light separated from the lens reduces strobe-induced back scatter and offers a variety of better light angles.

Make the most of your adjustments using the f-stop feature on the camera. With lots of available light, use settings of f/8 or f/11. As the light decreases, use f/5.6 or f/4. Remember, as you lower the f-stop the

105

depth-of-field is decreased, making your focus and distance estimating critical. The f-stop setting also affects the "sun ball" visible in the background when you shoot upward; the lower the f-stop, the larger the ball (the f/4 ball is huge). If you have some doubt about your settings, err on the side of underexposure (f/8 or higher). A photo lab can do a lot more with an underexposed image than it can with a burned-out, overexposed one.

For a flooded camera, first remove the batteries to limit major corrosion damage. Next, flush with fresh water as soon as possible. Follow with a flush of a small amount of alcohol to remove the water. Then blow-dry the camera with a hair dryer set on "low." Continue to work the shutter throughout the drying process. Once the camera is dry, immediately seal it in a plastic bag and send it to a repair facility.

TIPS FROM THE EXPERTS

"It's important to do research before attempting bluewater photography," says James D. Watt. "Study your subject, learn where it can be found and under what conditions. Once in the water, try to descend before your subject sees you and avoid eye contact. Good freediving skills contribute more to the production of outstanding bluewater images than do photographic skills."

Bill Boyce suggests setting your f-stop, shutter speed and focus in advance; then leave them alone and be patient. Wait for your subject to become centered and within the focus range. Make a few well-composed shots rather than many sloppy ones. Panning shots, for moving fish, should be taken as if you are skeet shooting. Pan at the same speed your subject is moving. Keep panning as you squeeze the shutter, and continue following your subject for a few seconds after you shoot. The best way to get good sun-ray pictures is to use speeds 1/125 or faster.

Phil Colla recommends that you keep the process simple and think ahead about what you are likely to encounter. This is especially true for freediving shots when bottom time is limited and shy subjects may offer only one chance.

Phil offers these additional points:

Keep it simple. Housed still cameras enable more accurate framing, automatic film advance, autofocus and a huge selection of lenses. But the learning curve adds complication to an otherwise simple shooting scenario. "I recall a true once-in-a-lifetime pass: 16 humpback whales swimming tightly together, pectoral fin to pectoral fin. I cranked off ten shots with my Nikonos-V with its 15-millimeter lens, all with acceptable manual exposure and fixed focus. Beside me, in perfect position, was another fellow using a more complicated camera—he missed much of the opportunity because the camera's autofocus (totally unnecessary) failed to lock on. High technology got in the way."

Bracketing. Bracketing refers to the practice of overexposing half an f-stop and underexposing one full f-stop. This is especially important with slide film, where the margin for exposure error is relatively large. If the subject is important, and you have more than one opportunity, try to bracket.

Patience and proximity. One of the first rules of underwater photography is to "get close" in order to improve the clarity of your subject and add impact to the composition. With regard to timid bluewater animals, marine mammals and compliance with the Marine Mammal Protection and Endangered Species Act, a good policy is to give your subject the chance to come to you. Allow the curiosity of your subject to initiate contact. The approach may never come, but if it does, you will be rewarded with longer, more intimate encounters and much better image opportunities. The alternative rushed approach usually causes the subject to flee, and in the case of protected marine mammals, might violate anti-harassment laws.

We hope it's clear that freediving is an excellent method, sometimes the only method, to approach elusive or shy underwater life. Once you've mastered the basics of freediving, adding the discipline of underwater photography provides rewards that last well beyond the dive.

Both images of the giant seabass (top) and the spooky white seabass (bottom) were taken while freediving.

PHOTOS: TERRY MAAS

Freediving wildlife photographer Phil Colla captured this image of a California blue shark. He artfully washed the underside of the shark with his strobe, complementing perfectly the sun's effect.

Underwater hockey

If you love the water, enjoy team play and are looking for a way to stay in excellent shape, then underwater hockey is your sport.

Originally played by freedivers to stay in shape during the winter months, underwater hockey has developed into a highly organized and competitive sport over the last 15 years. This lively sport enjoys national and international recognition. To help us explain the basics, we've interviewed Kendall Banks and Tim Burke, two nationally recognized competitors with world championship experience. Tim was the 1996 Underwater Society of America's Underwater Hockey Athlete of the year. Kendall has served as National Underwater Hockey Director for the Underwater Society of America and has represented the United States eight times on the national team in world play; his teammates have elected him captain seven times.

Underwater hockey is loads of fun, but be forewarned: this is one tough sport. It's like running up and down a flight of stairs on a single breath, breathing again at the bottom of the stairs and then repeating this cycle for fifteen minutes. It is a high intensity, anaerobic sport that requires excellent physical fitness. "Although long breath-holds are helpful, they are not critical to success," Tim stresses. "It is more important to couple short, effective breath-hold times—enough to complete each play—with short surface intervals."

In underwater hockey, two teams of six, wearing only masks, fins and snorkels, compete in a swimming pool. Their objective is to drive the puck with short hockey sticks into their opponent's goal. "It is similar to ice hockey, where speed, puck control, passing and awareness of others is critical," says Tim. "Yet it is played on the bottom of a swimming pool while you hold your breath."

National and international competitions consist of 10 designated players—six in the water and four substitutes. A player can be substituted at any time but this must occur in certain designated areas, and the exiting player must be completely out of the water before the substitute can enter. Violate this rule and you get a one-minute penalty for "substitution foul," leaving your remaining five teamates extremely vulnerable.

National championships occur yearly and the venue rotates around the country. World championships are held every other year. It may take up to two weeks of elimination contests to determine the world champions. The Australians have dominated the men's division from 1988 through the late 90s. Other strong contenders represent South Africa, Canada, New Zealand, France, Britain, Netherlands and the United States. While some countries heavily subsidize their teams, American players typically pay their own expenses. This makes it difficult to consistently field top talent. The average age of the American competitor is 35, compared to 25 in most other countries. This may be due, in part, to financial considerations. Also, the sport isn't as well-known in the United States as it is in other countries, where most people are

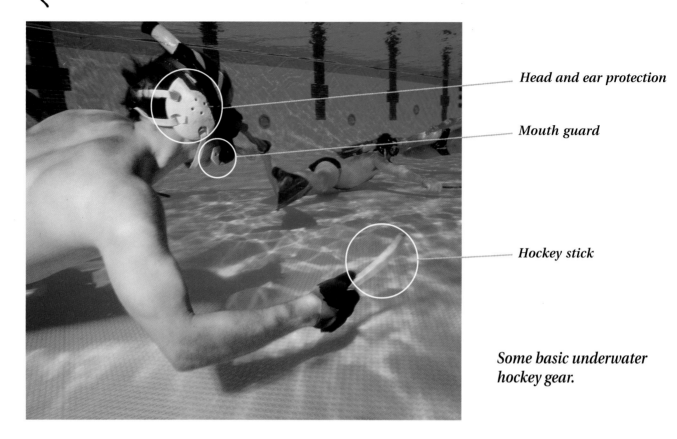

Head and ear protection

Mouth guard

Hockey stick

Some basic underwater hockey gear.

introduced to the sport in school.

A game consists of two 15-minute halves, separated by a three-minute half time. There are three referees—one deck referee and two underwater referees, one of whom places the puck in the center of the pool. The deck referee, or chief referee, whistles the start of the game. Teams aligned along the side of the pool send players called "forwards" swimming free-style to the middle, where they dive to gain control of the puck. The other players arrange themselves into positions or zones—often three forwards and three backs. "This sport is definitely a team sport requiring each player to play their assigned positions," says Kendall. "My greatest thrills stem from the successful completion of a play made possible by the perfect coordination of the whole team's effort."

The pool is typically 25 yards (22.7 meters) in length and 6 to 10 feet (2 to 3 meters) deep. While a pool with a flat bottom is preferred, slanting pools are acceptable because teams rotate sides at half-time. Ten-foot (3-meter) metal goals are centered at each end of the pool. They're made with a shallow backstop and a 4-inch (10-centimeter) trough. To register a goal, you must either hit the backstop with

your puck or it must land in the trough. Once a goal is scored, each team has 30 seconds to return to its side of the pool. This means that the scoring team must swim back 25 yards (22.7 meters), regroup and send in substitutes all within 30 seconds before the whistle sounds again. Late players must touch their end of the pool before resuming play; if they do not, they receive a one-minute penalty.

The rules are simple: no standing on the pool bottom or blatant fouling (holding or grabbing another). Although incidental contact does occur, underwater hockey is still considered a non-contact sport. Are there any risks? Sure—blackout from over-exertion, broken noses and teeth from puck-passing and ruptured eardrums from fin slaps are possible, but rare; and, in most cases, preventable with the use of proper gear. The most common injuries are bruises and cuts on the knees and knuckles caused by striking the pool bottom or being hit by sticks and pucks.

The gear required to play underwater hockey is minimal. "All you need are mask, fins, snorkel, a glove, hockey stick, head and ear protection, a mouth guard and a good roll of duct-tape," says Kendall. "You can purchase most of the special gear from the

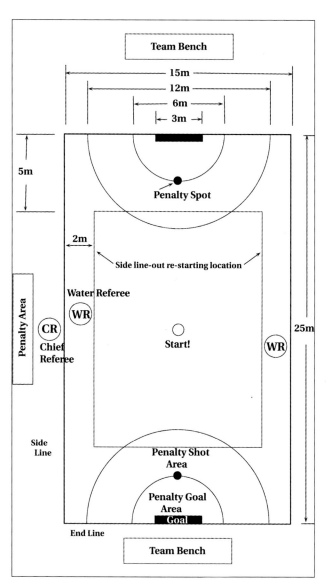

The court layout for underwater hockey.

Team Bench

15m

12m

6m

3m

5m

Penalty Spot

2m

Side line-out re-starting location

Water Referee

WR

Penalty Area

CR

Chief Referee

Start!

WR

25m

Side Line

Penalty Shot Area

Penalty Goal Area

Goal

End Line

Team Bench

dislodged due to accidental contact. Masks made with two smaller lenses separated by a plastic frame are best because they offer greater protection against breakage when an errant puck strikes your face. Avoid masks that have a high volume and a large, single faceplate.

Use white cotton or orange fish cleaning gloves that you customize yourself. Simply put your hand in the glove, spread silicone sealant over the top, making sure that you cover your knuckles and fingers. Sealants or adhesives such as RTV, 3M 5200 Marine Adhesive and GE Silicone-II work well. As the material cures, hold your hockey stick to make the correct contour for the glove.

Hockey sticks are generally made of wood or sometimes plastic. They are required to float when they fall out of your hand. You normally purchase sticks in pairs: one white, the other black to differentiate the teams. Because the dimensions of the stick are strictly regulated, be sure to consult the USofA regulations before you take the time and money to make them. Some players attach their sticks to their wrists with lanyards to retain them in the event they become dislodged. If you choose to use

A good mask for underwater hockey has two small lenses encased in a plastic frame. Note the snorkel with its taped-in-place mouth guard.

Underwater Society of America (USofA)." Use duct-tape for field repairs or for securing fins to your feet.

Shorter than the long freediving fins, hockey fins trade top-end speed for better maneuverability. Avoid hard, sharp fins because they can injure other divers. Popular fins include the Mare's HP and the Avanti-L. Other fins are available from Cressi Sub, U.S. Divers and Dacor. Because players have been known to cheat by pulling off their opponents' fins, and other players sometimes lose their fins in radical turns, many top hockey players employ fin keepers. Some use fixie poms while others prefer the absolute security of fins bound to their feet with duct-tape.

Use a low-volume, easy-to-clear mask; divers frequently need to clear their masks, which become

Kendall Banks (left) and Yori Huyah (below) demonstrate "getting some air" with their pucks.

a lanyard, make sure that it's stretchable for easy removal in an emergency.

One player made the mistake of fashioning a lanyard from a nylon cord that fit snugly to her hand. During a play she almost passed out and drowned when her stick became wedged in one of the metal grates that covers the drain on the bottom of the pool. After several attempts, the panic-stricken player luckily removed her hand from the lanyard and rushed to the surface for air.

Pucks used during regulation play weigh approximately 3 pounds (1.36 kilograms) and consist of a lead core coated in a hard, protective plastic shell. Players abandoned uncoated lead years ago when

they found it caused unsightly black blemishes on the bottom of the pool. You can purchase pucks from the USofA for approximately $50 apiece.

Head gear, an important piece of safety equipment, is used to prevent facial injuries and ruptured eardrums. The plastic guard dissipates pressure that would otherwise cause a "water hammer" effect to an ear by a fin slap or an abrasion to your cheek by a puck or stick strike. While water polo caps are the most common choice for head gear, some players have recently begun experimenting with wrestling helmets, which appear to work well. Remember to evaluate the possibility of increased drag when you choose your head gear.

112

Play action: teammate on the far right dives down to anticipate a pass from a diver who needs to go up for air.

Finally, don't forget your mouth guard. It is made from the chin strap of a roller blade helmet cut to fit around the mouthpiece of your snorkel. Duct-tape is often used to secure it in place. The mouth guard is the newest piece of safety equipment mandated by the USofA because there have been several occasions where divers required extensive dental treatment after receiving a blow to the mouth from a puck.

Tim is quick to offer some advice to beginners. "Keep your stick out in front of you at all times, limit your breath-hold times to short, effective durations and otherwise follow the play on the surface," he says. "Work on puck-handling, shooting and curling. Coordinate the timing of your surface dive to anticipate the play and your teammates. Improve your physical conditioning by swimming with and without fins."

You can locate the closest underwater hockey team in your area by contacting the USofA or your local dive shop. Because teams are always looking for new players, they often recruit by conducting training seminars and demonstrations. We're confident that you will find this sport exciting, and an excellent way to stay in shape during the "off season."

Members of opposite teams contest for control of the puck. Be prepared for some exciting team play and one-on-one action.

Stacy Kim (right) defends a curl from Bridgit Grimm.

Monofins

Monofin swimmers, equipped with special front-mounted snorkels, bear a striking likeness to marine mammals—especially dolphins, who must appreciate the resemblance as well because the two often play together for hours.

In 1967, Siberian Russians invented the monofin by riveting two traditional rubber fin pockets to a single blade of metal. For almost two decades the Russians would dominate the sport of fin swimming, one aspect of which is a 50-meter underwater race.

Monofins provide freedivers with a powerful yet graceful alternative to the standard pair of fins. They are used for serious fin swimming competitions as well as for open-ocean excursions. We'll begin this chapter with comments from Mike Gower, president of the Underwater Society of America (US of A)and Director of Fin Swimming Competitions. Then we'll profile two expert amateur monofin swimmers: competitor and coach Peppo Biscarini, whose contributions have advanced the sport, and Theresa Villa, who gracefully interacts with marine mammals.

Mike Gower talks excitedly about monofin swimming events. "Racers in the 50-meter apnea event generate an awesome 6-inch pressure-wave riding across the pool as they pass underwater," he says. "The wave is shaped like a 'V' because the fastest swimmers get center positions in the pool and form the tip of a wedge-shaped wave."

Monofin-equipped swimmers routinely clock 13-minute miles over the water in long-distance races. Over or under the water, they're the world's fastest swimmers. Some reach speeds of 7.5 miles-per-hour (12.2 kilometers-per-hour).

According to Gower, monofins benefit both swimmers and freedivers. The speed monofins generate helps conventional competitive swimmers learn to streamline their bodies. For freedivers, monofins offer an invigorating new diving experience.

Freedivers using monofins pay a price for the increased speed. Mike estimates that for the 25 percent increase in speed, they expend 25 percent more energy than conventional fin users. This is because monofins emphasize the larger muscles of the thigh and the abdomen, which use more oxygen than the smaller calf muscles emphasized in the standard fin stroke. Still, because of the more efficent use of muscles, a diver equipped with a monofin may swim further underwater on a single breath than a diver using two fins.

The first major fin swimming competition took place in Italy in 1967. It was not until 1980, however, that the relatively new sport received a major boost with arrival of Italian-born Peppo Biscarini. At age 15, Peppo smashed the previous 24-hour, long-distance swimming world record, covering the previous distance in just 21 hours. As he kicked on his back, his support team fed him fluids and raw horsemeat. His 83.7- kilometer record held for 6 years. In 1982, the United States participated in its first international competition, in Santa Clara, California. In 1987, Peppo won three gold medals and set three national records at the first United States National Fin Swimming Championships.

Peppo Biscarini (above) demonstrates his award-winning form.

National champion Chris Morgan (left) leaps free from the water like a dolphin with powerful monofin strokes.

In Europe, Peppo studied the use of the fin and contributed to the design of a new generation of monofins. Later he promoted the monofin as a teaching aid for conventional swimmers. Biscarini felt that when American swimmers were introduced to the monofin, they, too, would appreciate its merits.

Biscarini supports the fin and the special front-mounted snorkel as excellent teaching aids for swimmers. Because of the increased speed, the fins improve technique by helping swimmers and divers to find a posture presenting the least hydrodynamic drag. Adapting to the fins automatically promotes streamlining.

Current monofins employ fiberglass for the blade. Two-millimeters thick at its base, the blade tapers to 0.72 millimeters at the tip. Subtle channels in the center guide the water toward the back, away from the sides where it spills off uselessly. A progressive taper encourages a laminar flow toward the back. Monofins are made in two configurations, depending on their use. For long distances, swimmers prefer a flexible blade. They use a somewhat shorter, stiffer blade for sprints.

Early in the history of fin-swimming competitions, swimmers with two fins began to lose to monofin-equipped swimmers. Two blades cause more turbulence and shed more water off the sides at high speeds. Sprinting single-blade fin users soon discovered that the fins caused so much thrust that they could not move their hands fast enough to keep up with the increased speed. Only toward the end of longer-course events do swimmers supplement their fin kicks with arm strokes.

Monofin swimmers and divers use a front-mounted snorkel to facilitate increased speed—the typical side-mounted snorkel vibrates and gets swept backwards. Exiting the mouth, the short snorkel extends up and over the nose to terminate just above the head. Tight straps hold it firmly and help prevent vibration.

Snorkel training benefits swimmers by promoting deeper and more efficient respiration. It also helps increase tolerance to carbon dioxide levels and may raise your "lactate threshold"—the point at which painful lactic acid builds faster in your muscles than you can clear it. Peppo, because of his freediver's background, feels that tolerance to carbon dioxide requires both mental and physical adaptation. Although sprint swimmers have enough oxygen available in their body stores to complete an under-water sprint, the pain associated with building levels of carbon dioxide causes a "carbon dioxide wall" that untrained swimmers and divers cannot tolerate.

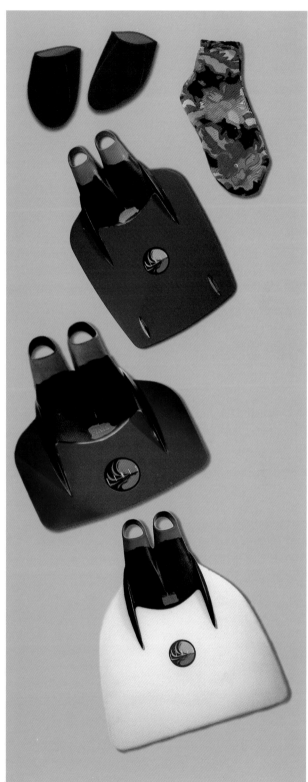

PHOTO: COURTESY FINIS

Monofin gear—fins and boots.

117

PHOTO: NORBERT WU

Monofin swimmers and divers use a front-mounted snorkel to facilitate increased speed.

PHOTO: COURTESY OF FINIS

Monofin-equipped divers actually swim faster underwater than on the surface. Compared to surface swimming, in which one-half of the blade's stroke is muted by the water-air interface, underwater swimming develops full force on both the up and down strokes of the blades.

Divers use a modified dolphin kick for power and streamlining. They extend their arms forward over their heads, often locking their hands together in a knife-cutting wedge. This arms-forward position rounds off the otherwise abrupt edge where the shoulders meet the trunk. Together the arms, trunk and legs oscillate in the vertical plane. Pivoting at the hips and assisted by powerful hip muscles, the stroke increases in amplitude and motion from minimal arm movement to maximal deflection at the fin tips.

When you ask Peppo about his most memorable freediving experience, he's quick to answer with stories of wild dolphin encounters. On a research trip to the Bahamas with eight Olympic swimmers, scientists tested the acceptance of "super swimmers" by dolphins. Peppo, using his monofin, was always first in the water. The dolphins quickly adopted these "human dolphins." Once, a proud dolphin mother maneuvered her baby between Peppo and herself so that the two adults swam sandwiching the young dolphin between them. Another time, Peppo tested his speed against the dolphins. One joined him in a belly-to-belly formation. Pressure pulses from the powerful dolphin just inches away beat against Peppo as the two swam for over 100 feet in formation.

Theresa Villa swims and dives with dolphins every week from the beaches of the Big Island of Hawaii. On a good day, she may interact with them for hours. For Theresa, it's the monofin that helps her sever her terrestrial bounds, and for a short while she becomes more dolphin than human.

Theresa is a powerful swimmer. As a young child, she watched her elder siblings compete in frigid South Dakota swim meets. At age 6, she held fast to her dad's back as he pulled her underwater. She entered her first competition at age 9. Her specialty

PHOTOS: TERRY MAAS

Theresa Villa (above) and Jennifer Veltmann (below)
swim with monofins in the blue waters of Hawaii.

is the butterfly stroke, with its strong, dolphin-kick component.

Theresa competed throughout college, then moved to Alaska. On her first Hawaiian vacation, she became captivated by the warm, clear water. Each day she swam further into the bay, shedding her natural fears of sharks and open water. Eight years later she returned to Alaska from her "vacation" to collect her belongings.

One day Theresa spotted a strange looking single-bladed fin—a monofin—on the beach. She asked its owner for a test ride. "It was an instant obsession," she recalls. "Putting on the trappings of a dolphin made me feel as if I had actually become one."

Competing with the monofin was a natural for Theresa. In 1996, she won three national fin swimming championship events and set three national records. Even more than she loves competition, she treasures

PHOTO: TERRY MAAS

PHOTO: ROGER HEATH

Theresa Villa swims with spinner dolphins off the island of Hawaii.

With fin-slaps on the surface, Theresa calls the dolphins to play.

her dolphin friends. She frequently swims with the same pod and recognizes individuals. She credits the monofin's dolphin-like appearance as a key to her dolphin interactions, but she's quick to recognize the dolphin's superior speed and agility. "They choose to swim with me—it's their decision," she says.

Theresa is a massage therapist. She comforts and heals people with her hands. So it was no surprise that a dolphin with a large open sore on its back split off from a pod to join her. Extending her right hand on the surface, she made small circular motions to send healing messages 30 feet (9 meters) below. The sick dolphin circled below in exact coordination with her hand. After a short while, it seemed satisfied and rejoined the pod.

Freediving with playful intelligent marine mammals is one of nature's all-time highs. When a wild group of animals invites you to join in their games, you cannot resist. While filming Theresa and her friend Jennifer Veltmann for the companion video to this book, Terry joined the two women in a dolphin game—"pass the leaf."

The first of six dolphin approached with a bright yellow leaf pinned firmly to its pectoral fin by water pressure. As it swam by, it flicked the leaf off with a pass to the dolphin behind, which deftly juggled the leaf from its nose to its dorsal fin to its fluke (tail) and finally off to us.

Theresa picked up the leaf with her usual grace and speed and then swam with the playful animals, enticing them with the leaf held between her fingers. The game finished its cycle when Theresa dropped the leaf and another wild dolphin picked it up with its pectoral fin. What a rush!

It's wonderful that successful amateur athletes such as Peppo and Theresa prize their dolphin-swimming experiences above all others. It's clear that the shape of the monofin, its motion underwater and the impressive increase in speed it provides makes this the ultimate dolphin-swimming accessory.

We asked Theresa to end this chapter with a description of her dolphin experiences:

Because I strive to live in the moment, each of my swims is extraordinary. On this day, piercing shafts of shimmering light rays dance in the silken blue ocean depths. I am monofinning through the calm named the "Pacific." After a wonderfully leisurely one-half mile, I glimpse movement of something in the water. Slowly, six dolphins materialize in a pod below me. They are resting. After spending long minutes at the sandy ocean bottom, they rise as one organism and catch short breaths before returning to the protected below. I wait patiently for them on the surface. As they move slowly to the surface, I feel a purity of being and oneness with these mammals. The moment is all that exists as I surrender to the feeling of peace and harmony. After dolphin-kicking toward them, I find myself accepted into the pod by their magical closeness. Enveloped in the wondrousness of the moment, I sense the pod's movement downward, and as part of the pod, I go with them.

Where they go, I go. I dive to my limits. I sense the temperature of my skin—warm at the surface, cooling on descent—as the calm of the deep pervades my being. I surprise myself by reaching the ocean bottom along

VIDEO CLIP: *The Joy of Freediving* BY TERRY MAAS AND LASZLO PAL.

Dolphins engage Theresa in a game of "pass the leaf."

with the pod and I rest with them. Finding a human swimmer at this depth seems to surprise the dolphins, as well. Mentally, I reassure them that everything is okay, that I just want to be there with them.

Hovering above the floor of the Pacific Ocean with spinner dolphins, I am wholly at peace. Relaxing into the reality of the moment, my need to breathe vanishes. My gaze shifts from the dolphins, to the horizontal line of sand and coral surrounding me, to the vertical view of clear water appearing to send light beams in my direction.

An internal calling to ascend reminds me of my own mammalian limits. With relaxed swishes of my dolphin tail, I send myself on a slow, free ride—an uplifting, an ascension. As I near the transition to air, elevating through each warming layer of water, I can see my growing reflection in the undersurface of the calm blue. The palpable surface tension first pulls at the top of my head, then my face and neck pass through. I notice conflicting physical sensations in my body—my head is heavy while the rest of my body floats freely. The dichotomy prevails— after all, I am a land creature in the water.

Game gathering

From the beginning of time, man has hunted the oceans of the world for food. Imagine the legions of world-class divers preceding us—their prowess evident in archaeological digs of fish bones and shells.

The tradition continues today. Native freedivers in the Bahamas and the South Pacific teach their children the art of gathering game from the ocean. In the deep, cold waters of Japan, *ama* divers harvest oysters. In every ocean of the world, freediving sportsmen hunt the sea, preferring the thrill of the experience and the fresh taste of their game to the task of buying pre-packaged fish in the supermarket.

We believe that, in most instances, freediving is the most sportsmanlike and environmentally sound way to hunt—in many countries it's the only legal method. Many locales limit spearfishing to freediving. Freediving is the only method by which you may take abalone in Northern California and lobsters in South Africa.

In this chapter, we'll examine the basics for gathering abalone, lobster and fish. Before you use any of these techniques, be sure that you study local fish-and-game laws for regulations that apply to freediving: acceptable methods, seasons, sizes and eligible species.

ABALONE

Because of their rich taste and relative scarcity worldwide, abalone have skyrocketed in price from a few dollars a pound in the 70s to over eighty dollars in 1997, when a moratorium was placed on the commercial take of these shellfish. While the abalone population in Southern California has suffered from over-fishing and withering-foot disease (a progressive wasting of the animal's body), their populations are healthy and abundant in Northern California. Some of the nation's best freedivers developed their skills while hunting abalone.

The red abalone of Northern California prefer an environment rich in oxygen and seaweed. Consequently, you'll find them in rough, surging areas, generally accompanied by limited visibility, in water from chest-deep to 40 feet (12 meters). While it's possible to find "abs" in the open, most hide in cracks or under rocks. In these cases, an underwater light and sharp eyes help make the catch.

An abalone unclasps its shell to feed. It raises up off its rocky perch with its single foot and gathers seaweed. If you bump its shell or cast a shadow over an abalone, it will quickly clamp its shell down with enough force to hold a diver underwater. Fortunately, we've never heard of such an incident, but be warned: an abalone requires considerable force to dislodge once it becomes alerted. It's best to sneak up on a feeding abalone and deftly slip your "ab iron" under its foot and quickly pry it loose.

Because you can fatally injure an undersized abalone with your iron, it's important to keep the iron under the tough foot of the animal—don't jab into its side. Abalone have a poor coagulation system and can bleed to death from a nick from an errant abalone iron.

PHOTO: TERRY MAAS

Ron Mullins prepares to "pop" a California abalone.

To help minimize injury to abalone, fish-and-game laws specify certain sizes and shapes for irons. Basically, they need to have rounded, smooth ends and flat bodies. You must measure your shell for the minimum size. It's best to pre-measure an abalone before you "pop" it loose.

Replace an undersized abalone where you found it (preferably the exact spot), and protect it long enough so that it may safely reattach. If you are not careful, the abalone may fall over or a fish might dislodge it.

We suggest you find an experienced abalone diver to help you shuck the animal from its shell. After removing the animal's gut sack, you'll slice the foot into 1/4-inch slabs that you pound with an abalone mallet until tender. Coat the patties in egg batter followed by bread crumbs, and fry each side in butter for 60 seconds. Save any trimmings; they make an excellent base for abalone chowder.

LOBSTER

You can find lobster on both coasts of the United States and in most tropical waters. In the North Atlantic, divers must battle the formidable "clawed lobster," known as the North American lobster or the Maine lobster. The Southern portions of the Atlantic and the Caribbean are home to the swift "spiny-lobster." Meanwhile, Pacific Coast divers enjoy its close relative, also called the spiny lobster.

The only extra gear you need to catch these delectable animals are a sturdy pair of gloves, a catch bag, a measuring device and a valid lobster license. Divers in the Atlantic and Caribbean may also use tickle sticks, snares and nets as fishing aids. Pacific Coast game laws limit divers' gear to their hands and stealth; no other aids are allowed. Use tickle sticks made from metal, fiberglass or an old spearshaft to coax lobsters out of their holes by nudging them on their sides. In most locales, it's illegal to spear lobsters, so be careful not to puncture the shell. The exception to this rule is in the Bahamas, where freedivers may spear lobsters with a pole spear or a Hawaiian sling.

Lobsters are nocturnal—they come out of their dens to scavenge for food at night. During the day, they hide among the rocks, cracks and crevices of the reef, under debris and wreckage or they simply burrow in the mud. Generally, the first you'll see of the lobster is its early-warning system—two long antennae waving from its shelter. These pressure-sensitive organs recognize potential predators by feel and by chemical changes in the water.

When you find a lobster, try to evaluate its home for a back entrance or neighbors such as moray eels. Normally, you'll make a swift grab and pin the lobster down with one hand while you grab its main body with the other. Sometimes it may be necessary to wait for them to fatigue or use a bit of finesse to pull them out. Other times, you can spook them into your hand by strategically positioning it at the "back door" of the lobster's home.

Avoid grabbing only the antennae or the claws of lobsters because the animal will readily jettison them into your hands as they flip backward in escape. Although lobsters have the ability to regenerate new appendages, they do so at the expense of the growth of the rest of their body, leaving them vulnerable to other predators. In the case of the Maine lobster, with claws powerful enough to severly crush a finger, try to pin both claws back together with one hand while you grab its body with the other.

PHOTO: TERRY MAAS

Gerald Lim finds a spiny lobster in a hole on the side of a vertical wall.

Be sure to turn your catch over and look for females bearing red eggs. Immediately place "berried" lobsters back in the reef unharmed. Use your gauge to measure the length of the carapace (the large body shell) from the eye socket to its rear end at the beginning of the tail. If it's a "keeper," place it into your bag tail first so that if it slips free, it will flap back into the bag. If it's short, you must release it immediately. Once you are out of the water, be sure to keep your lobsters cool and moist until you are ready to cook them. A cooler filled with ice and seaweed works well.

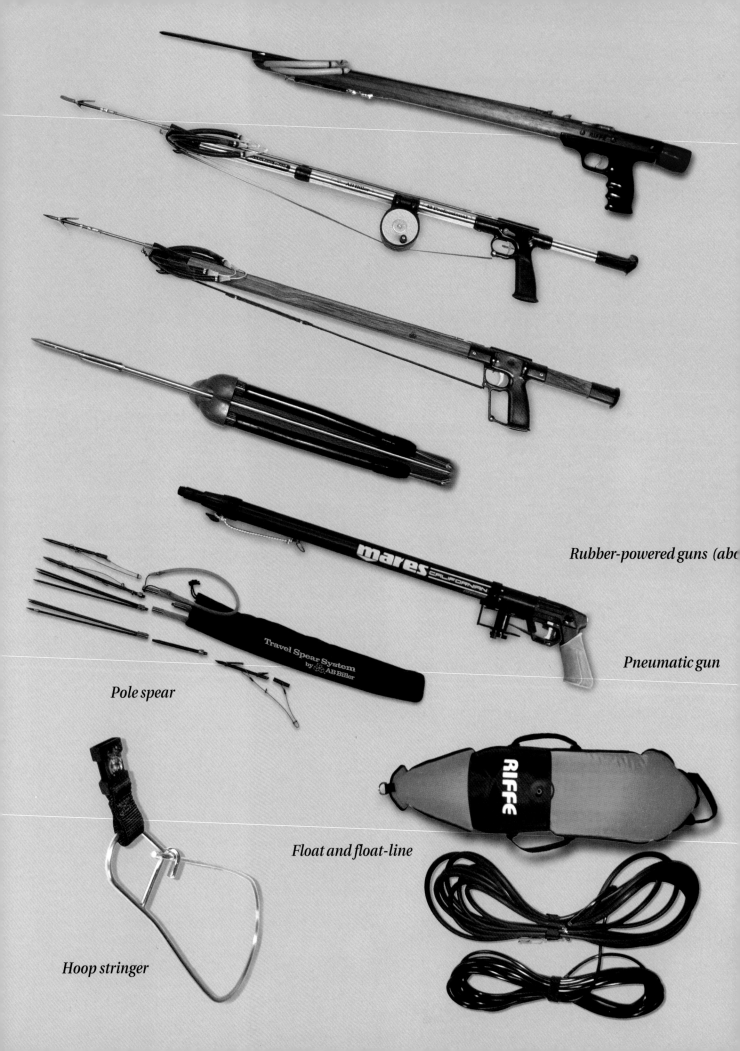

Rubber-powered guns (ab[...]

Pneumatic gun

Pole spear

Float and float-line

Hoop stringer

SPEARFISHING

If you like to fish or hunt and swim underwater, then spearfishing is for you. Both the diver who hunts for dinner and the purist who lays on the ocean bottom for long minutes waiting to see just one trophy-sized striper or white seabass agree that the challenge of locating and stalking fish in their own environment is intoxicating. Besides providing fresh fish for dinner, spearfishers experience an intense communion with the underwater world. Living in the moment, spearfishers see and feel what casual observers miss—the ocean's pulse, subtle changes in currents, apprehension of baitfish and a whole host of interactions among the sea's creatures. Imagine swimming for hours with manta rays and whale sharks, coming bill-to-speargun with colorful sailfish and giant marlin, observing natural predator-and-prey relationships or experiencing the thrill of spearing and landing a record gamefish.

Even though the sport of spearfishing was largely responsible for the birth of freediving, it has become a controversial activity. Because of its high beach visibility, the excesses of a few and the ecology movement, spearfishers have come under attack by those who do not understand the sport. In many countries spearfishing is a tremendously popular sport, enjoyed by those who consider their top "spearos" to be national celebrities. This is due in part to cultural tradition and laws that make spearfishing with scuba gear illegal. In Southern Europe, freediving and spearfishing have evolved into a totally unique and separate sport supported by equipment manufacturers, magazines dedicated to freediving and the general public.

Spearfishing has the potential to be the most environmentally sound method of harvesting fish. While responsible anglers practice "catch and release," spearfishers "release and catch"—they take only the fish they want while letting the others swim by. A spearfisher can easily discriminate species, size and sex. In the global scheme, spearfishers take relatively few fish. In California, for every 3,000 fish harvested from the sea, commercial fisherman take 2,800, anglers 200 and spearfishers less than one. Still, spearfishers can make a significant negative impact by the way they behave in such high-visibility areas as public beaches and boat ramps.

Today there is a new breed of spearfisher— young men and women with new diving technology and an old-school "purist" attitude. They shoot only what they need for dinner. To lessen their environmental impact, they study the life histories of their quarry, avoid slow-growing species, increase their spearfishing areas to reduce localized negative impacts, target blue-water species rather than reef fish and constantly increase their level of skill and knowledge.

In our opinion, freediving is an excellent way to enjoy the ocean and to hunt fish. Successful spearfishers rely on their stealth and the fish's natural curiosity to make their catch. While a freediver might have just a minute underwater, this disadvantage is usually offset by his silent, unobtrusive entry into the fish's world. For a brief moment the freediver becomes part of the environment, joining the ocean's endless food web.

So how do you learn spearfishing, what gear do you need and how do you locate and stalk fish? Finding a buddy who knows how to spearfish is an excellent way to start. To locate spearfishing diving clubs in your area, contact your local dive shop or the Underwater Society of America.

Spearfishing gear

Spearfishing does not require a garage full of gear—all you need are a pole spear or speargun, a float, gloves to handle fish, a knife to dispatch your catch and a stringer to secure it. In spite of the basic simplicity of the gear, however, spearfishers have an enormous array of equipment to choose from. Your professional dive center can help you obtain the proper equipment for your local conditions.

Beginning with a pole spear is an excellent way to learn spearfishing. Because of the spear's limited range, 1 to 5 feet (0.3 to 1.5 meters), you've got to learn stalking and fish habits—what frightens them and what makes them curious. Pole spears are a simple and effective tool to land small fish up to 10 pounds— rockfish living in cracks and crevices or bottom-dwelling species such as halibut.

The Hawaiian sling is another excellent choice for the beginner, or for anyone who appreciates a challenge. It resembles a slingshot where the spear shaft is propelled through a tube of wood, plastic or metal powered by a surgical-rubber sling. You hold the tube with one hand and stretch the sling and spear back with the other. The released, unattached spear becomes a free-flying arrow. Hawaiian slings are effective on small, open-water gamefish up to 15 pounds (7 kilograms) and some larger fish, such as groupers, that tend to "hole up" after being shot. Since Hawaiian slings use a free shaft, they're most

PHOTO: TERRY MAAS

*Ron Mullins heads to the surface
with a California white seabass.*

effective in clear water. Practice with a target so you can make perfect kill shots. Hawaiian slings are most popular in Florida and the Caribbean.

Most people prefer a speargun for underwater fishing. Since each section of the country presents different conditions, and each diver has his own style and method for fishing, manufacturers make a variety of spearguns. No one gun will serve all purposes. You've got two basic choices: guns propelled by air pressure and guns propelled by rubber. The pneumatic gun is powered by compressed air, while the band gun is powered by stretched surgical-rubber tubing. The ideal barrel length for most conditions is 36 to 42 inches (90 to 100 cm). A well-made gun should include a stainless steel trigger mechanism, heat-treated, spring-steel spearshafts, and a barrel that will float after the shaft is fired.

Domestic manufacturers AB Biller Co., Riffe and JBL make excellent all-round spearfishing guns. European-made guns are generally lighter and quicker than their United States counterparts. Because of their speed and accuracy they are excellent for smaller reef fish. Beuchat, Esclapez, Mares and Picasso all make quality guns. Alexander and Riffe supply larger guns for open-water bluewater species such as tuna and wahoo. For details on these types of guns and bluewater hunting see Terry's book, *Bluewater Hunting and Freediving*.

For practice, take your new gun to a calm, clear body of water and shoot at targets. A buoy or milk container suspended 3 feet (1 meter) off the bottom works well. In just a few hours, you'll learn the dynamics of loading and firing, and you'll have a good idea about the gun's effective power and range. You will learn more about your gun in one hour of target shooting than you can in a full dive season.

When you are spearfishing, pay close attention to the way you swim with your speargun since it is another major source of drag. You may grab it by the muzzle and swim with your arms outstretched using the "superman" position. Some spearfishers prefer to hold the handle of the speargun in a reverse grip and then place their arms along their side—the gun rests on your shoulder with the barrel and shaft parallel to your head. Compared to the typical two-handed hunting pose, these two techniques should help spearfishers gain precious bottom time.

Terminal gear helps you recover a fish that has disappeared into a cave or off into the blue with your spear or sometimes your speargun. While some spearfishers use a reel attached to their gun, we prefer a floating trail-line that attaches the spear to the float. Reels add bulk to the gun; they may cause the gun to sink and they often backlash or tangle.

Trail lines may be as simple as a polypropylene cord or as complicated as a 100-foot (30-meter) elastic bungee. A simple tool to play the fish, the trail line offers a chance to re-rig the gun quickly and promotes safety. You attach a flagged buoy to one end and your spearshaft line to the other. If you feel that you are running out of air, you can simply drop the gun without worrying about losing it. Remember, no speargun is worth your life—drop it if you need to. With a trail line, it's a simple matter to recover it later. The trail line also serves as a good marker. If you find a cave entrance, you can mark the spot by dropping your gun and following the line back on your next dive.

You'll need a knife to manage line-tangle emergencies and to dispatch your catch. It is important to retrieve your fish and to still it, or "pith it," immediately. This helps prevent broken gear, injuries from a thrashing fish that can stick you with its fins and spines, escape of the fish or the attraction of unwanted predators such as sharks and barracudas.

Once you have taken your catch, you'll need to prepare it for transport. The safest solution is to immediately place it into your source of transportation: inner-tube, kayak or boat. Another possibility is to use fish stringers that help you carry your fish. Avoid game bags because they are bulky and awkward—a previously captured fish may escape when you attempt to put another in. If you dive in an area with sharks or barracudas, such as the Caribbean, you will want to place your catch immediately into a boat or dive kayak.

In Southern California or New England, it's common practice for divers to carry their fish with them until it's convenient to remove them from the water. A stringer composed of a steel pin and 2 to 3 feet (0.6 to .9 meters) of nylon line allows you to carry your fish over your shoulder or around your waist. This method works well since the fish do not interfere with your kicking. Some divers use a large, safety-pin stringer and attach it to their weight belt.

If you feel uneasy about swimming with your speared catch on your back, we suggest that you attach your fish stringer to your float and tow them. The safety-pin style stringer works best for towing on your float.

Gloves help protect you from the sharp parts of the fish—their spines, teeth and the gill rakers found inside their mouths. If the water is warm, use leather or cotton gloves; in colder areas use neoprene gloves.

Techniques

Finding and stalking fish is an art that you develop after years of observation and practice. Spearfishers improve with age because this sport is as dependent on experience, or "fish sense," as it is on physical ability. Fish behavior varies due to a myriad of factors: fish species, time of year, time of day, currents, tide, water visibility, food availability, water temperature and habitat. If you study each day you hunt and input each variable into the "computer of your mind," you'll soon develop fish sense: how, when, and where to find fish.

You hunt fish in three basic places: in their rocky homes, hiding in the sand or free swimming. Many desirable fish stay close to their caves. "Hole-fishing freedivers" search for reefs with the aid of a depth sounder or by listening for clicking rock shrimp and feeding fish.

PHOTO: PHILIPPE MURA

A European diver checks a promising cave.

Bottom fish usually swim close to their sheltering cave or lie perched on a nearby peak on the reef. When alerted, they quickly dodge into the deepest portion of their cave, where you might need a light to find them. If you find yourself needing to surface before locating the fish, leave your gun in front of the opening. This serves both as a marker for the cave opening and as a guard to prevent the fish from fleeing the cave.

Many fish, such as flounder and halibut, are masters of camouflage. Lying on the sand or nestled under a thin blanket of sand, they're difficult to spot.

PHOTO: TERRY MAAS

Gerald Lim with a deep-water whitefish.

Sometimes it's only two small eye bulges or a faint outline that gives them away. Other times, an explosion in the sand is the only clue you'll have that you just swam over a flatfish. In sandy areas, look for contrasting sand or fish parts such as an eye or a tail—don't expect to see the whole fish. Bottom fish often prefer sand edges along the sides of rocks, wreckage and sea grass.

After you have speared your fish, it's best to swim down the line to your shaft and grab it for the swim back up to the surface. In the event of a poor shot, this will prevent the fish from fighting off the shaft. Try keeping the fish "belly up" (causing tonic immobility—a trick used by many fish handlers), to prevent the fish from thrashing about.

The most difficult fish to hunt are the open-water reef and pelagic species. The only way you'll get close

to these oceanic speedsters is to appeal to their curiosity. Each species is different. One will swim close as you strum your spearbands like a bass guitar; others will vanish. Some are attracted to sounds that you make in your throat or will swim over to check out sand plumes you're generating by waving your hand over the bottom.

Terry once coaxed a wary white seabass within feet of him by "croaking"—a call made deep in the throat. He has also seen the same fish sprint away from the untimely squeak of his ear equalization. As a general rule, you'll do better by being quiet and unobtrusive.

Many divers descend in a hunt-like posture and then hover above the bottom looking for a fish. Often their quarry has already noticed them, and as the diver starts to move in its direction, the fish simply swims away, leaving the provoking question, "Do I have enough air to follow it?"

David prefers another method—"crashing to the bottom"—a technique that relies on the fish's natural curiosity. On the descent, instead of leveling off above the bottom, you dive straight down in a perfect vertical form. Once you reach the bottom, freeze in the hunting posture and wait. Hopefully, you'll see a fish in the distance watching you. Don't look at the fish directly since it may notice your eye movements. Keep it within your field of vision. If you remain quiet and still, chances are you'll be rewarded by a fish that approaches you.

Camouflage wetsuits made from variegated colors and patterns help you blend visually with the reef. Solid blue or green works best in open water. To avoid alerting the fish's sharp eye, make sure all of the colors on your gear are subdued—no whites or flashy metal. Fish are color blind but they accurately sense contrast and movement.

The best strategy to hunt free-swimming pelagic fish is to use what the Europeans call the "long wait." Basically, you'll swim suspended in midwater near the thermocline (a layer of water colder than the water above), or at the depth you've spotted fish before, and remain motionless and quiet. Hopefully, before you're too blue in the face, they will come into range. Because even the best speargun's effective range is rarely more than 15 feet (4.5 meters), you've got to get close.

Take care with your aim and avoid desperation shots. If you hit the fish in the spinal column, usually along its lateral line, you'll dispatch it immediately. Another target is the brain, but it's usually difficult to hit because of its small size. From the side, it's located directly behind the eye. From above, the brain can be found by locating the apex of an equilateral triangle with a line connecting the eyes as the base of the triangle, and the apex facing the tail in the middle of the top of the head. It is much easier to haul up a fish rendered motionless than one kicking and charging about, getting tangled in seaweed or rocks—and all the while ringing the dinner bell for sharks.

It's important to note the relationship between bottom topography and fish aggregations. Fish congregate around special structures on the reef or around any structure in a flat sandy area. The best way to hunt these areas is at the edges. Swimming to the middle of a "hot spot" and blasting away guarantees that thefish will scatter. Hunt at the edges and hide under or behind rocks and try coaxing the fish to you.

In the ocean, fish are a part of the great food web where life feeds on life and where most animals get eaten before they die of old age. Examining the stomach contents of your catch offers valuable clues as to what they are eating. California white seabass love squid; when you locate squid, white seabass will be near. South African "spearos" anxiously await the annual sardine invasion along their east coast for the tasty king mackerel that follow.

Many fish, like fowl, are seasonal migrators. Spearfishers in New England closely monitor the spring's rising water temperature for clues when the first striped bass will appear. In summer, they look for the warm waters of the gulf stream carrying such fish as giant bluefin tuna and mahi mahi.

More recently, bluewater hunters have been venturing away from the reefs into the bluewater, the wildest environment left on earth. While the risks are potentially greater—sharks, drowning, being lost at sea—so are the rewards. Interacting one-on-one with large oceanic creatures in the world's last remaining frontier is an experience you'll never forget.

Once you become proficient at hunting you may want to test yourself against others by competing in a spearfishing competition. Local eliminations determine eligibility for the national championships. Most meets consist of 30 minutes of travel time by any human-powered means—swimming, rowing, paddling—followed by 3 to 5 hours of freediving and spearfishing, with 30 minutes of travel time to return to the weigh-in area. Violate one of these rules and you'll get disqualified. Each diver is awarded a point per fish and a point per pound. The diver with the most points wins.

Contest organizers try to limit the effect on local reefs by frequently rotating the venue and spreading the competition zone over a large area. They

PHOTO: TERRY MAAS

Winners of the 1997 Long Beach Neptunes' Catalina bluewater meet: Gerald Lim (left) came in second, Ron Mullins (center) finished first and Bill Ernst placed third.

generally limit the number of fish allowed to below permissible fish-and-game bag limits, and they increase the eligible size of contest fish over fish-and-game minimums. These competitions will definitely test your mental and physical capabilities as well as provide you with an excellent forum for gaining further knowledge and techniques from top local divers.

Whether you hunt for fish, lobster or abalone, breath-hold diving certainly offers your quarry better odds than any other form of fishing. Just the thrill of the hunt and the companionship with other hunters is enough reward to compensate for those many days when you come home empty-handed. And when you're lucky, you can look forward to ending the day with a king's ransom—a meal of fresh seafood.

Bluewater hunters venture away from the reefs into the open ocean, the wildest environment left on earth. Above, Mark Barville hunts the waters of Guadalupe Island, Mexico for giant bluefin tuna. Greg Pickering (left) of Australia shows off a handsome native Spanish mackerel.

Diving for depth records

We want to be clear: competitive deep freediving is a dangerous sport, and we don't condone it. Divers, caught up in the frenzy to see who can dive the deepest, may end up taking irrational risks. Many have died. Still, the sport has produced many colorful figures, including a woman who is setting records at just 19 years old, a man who belches air from his stomach into his lungs as well as two epic rivalries. In spite of its danger—or maybe because of it—there is a lot to be learned from those who pursue this sport.

Individuals, supported by a team of trainers and safety divers, compete in three classes to see who's the deepest breath-hold diver in each class. Dives may take three minutes or more in the record attempt, and some reach depths in excess of 400 feet (122 meters). Only a handful of devoted divers around the world participate. Yet given the sport's growing media attention and the information we're obtaining about man's ultimate limits underwater, we feel compelled to address it. This chapter is intended to be a source of information only and not a substitute for proper training and experience.

Freediving for depth has been practiced for years in Europe. It gained popularity in the United States with the release of the 1988 film *The Big Blue*, which loosely depicted the life of freediving guru Jacques Mayol and his rivalry with Enzo Maiorca.

The first American deep freediver was United States Navy diver Robert Croft, who held the 1967 world record of 217 feet (66 meters). The current record is 439 feet (134 meters). More recently, there has been a resurgence of popularity in this esoteric sport due to the new rivalry of Francisco "Pipin" Ferreras and Umberto Pellizzari and the multitude of television events covering Pipin's record dives off the coasts of Mexico and Florida.

Diving for depth records takes an enormous amount of money, planning and technical support and the dangers are many. Divers experience temporary body distortions from the incredible effect of water pressure that makes a man's lungs compress to the size of his fist. They may collide with their scuba-equipped safety divers (there are several at multiple depths to aid the possibly distressed deep diver). They may lose contact with specialized equipment such as the sled or lift bag. They must contend with the unexpected: deep ocean currents, inability to equalize at the rapid ascent and descent rates, shallow water blackout or their under-estimation of depth and/or time.

The event coordinator must contend not only with the safety of the freediver but that of the safety divers equipped with sophisticated gear, who may be at greater risk. Because today's record depths are in excess of 400 feet, safety divers using special scuba gear, strategically located along the route, must use mixed gases to prevent judgment-destroying, intoxicating narcosis and avoid decompression illness. Many hours after the freediver surfaces and receives his accolades, the last safety divers surface after completing their lengthy decompressions. The logistics of organizing the site, the boats, special descent equipment and safety divers are simply enormous.

Keeping up with the records is just as difficult. In the 1970s, Mayol and Maiorca kept leap-frogging year after year as they battled fiercely for the ultimate title as the world's deepest man. Today Umberto Pellizzari and Pipin are vying for the same title.

There are three categories of deep freediving: constant-weight, variable-weight and no-limits. The constant-weight category is under the strict auspices of CMAS, the World Sub-Aquatics Activities Confederation. CMAS, recognized by the International Olympic Committee, is the oldest international federation ratifying diving activities. It started ratifying depth records in 1949 when Raimondo Bucher set the first record at 98 feet (30 meters).

Divers in the constant-weight category equip themselves with typical freediving gear. Under the power of their legs, they descend and ascend, keeping all of their equipment in place. They may not change volume nor may they add or drop equipment, including weights. The diver is not allowed to touch the descent line. The constant-weight record was previously held by Umberto Pellizzari who, in 1991, descended to 230 feet (70 meters). On Sept. 27, 1995, Corsican diver Eric Charrier smashed Pellizzari's record, reaching 241 feet (73.5 meters). He wore a 2-millimeter neoprene suit, a mask partially filled with a silicone component, a pair of fins specifically manufactured to match his physical capabilities and 4 pounds (1.8 kilograms) of lead.

In the second category, variable-weight, the diver may use ballast up to one-third of his body weight to help propel him downward. The maximum weight allowed for this type of dive is 66 pounds (30 kilograms). However, divers in this category must ascend back to the surface under their own power, either pulling themselves up the descent line and/or using their fins. The current record is 315 feet (96 meters). Ratified by the Italian Federation of Underwater Activities (F.I.P.S.), this record is held by Cuban-born Francisco, "Pipin" Ferreras.

In 1970, after Jacques Mayol's record dive to 250 feet (76 meters) in Japan, CMAS discontinued its endorsement of the variable-weight and no-limits record attempts because of the dangers to both the freediver and the safety diver. Further deep record attempts would be ratified as "experimental," for scientific research only. In 1991, despite the CMAS ruling, F.I.P.S., a member of CMAS, once again began to sanction the variable-weight category. However, these records are valid only in Italy.

Participants in the no-limits or absolute diving category may dive any way they like as long as they hold their breath. For the descent, they typically use a heavily ballasted sled, attached to the descent line; for the ascent, they use a buoyancy device—usually a lift bag filled with air from a compressed-air cylinder. The record is verified by a remote video camera attached to the end of the ballasted guide line. Modern sleds also employ an attached camera to monitor the diver. In this most extreme and dangerous category, freedivers reach incredible depths with astonishing speed. Typical records occur within 2 to 2 1/2 minutes compared to older records over 3 1/2 minutes. Although the no-limits category is not sanctioned by CMAS or F.I.P.S, current attempts loosely follow their safety rules.

Deep freedivers typically use high-performance equipment custom-fitted to their size and matched to their strength. To reduce drag, they use suits with smooth rubber exteriors. For the ultimate in propulsion power, many wear fins constructed of carbon fiber composites. The special fin blades are so fragile that when they hit the bottom or a reef, they shatter into pieces. To prevent squeeze, most divers don't wear face masks. The few divers who do wear masks generally fill them with a silicone-base material to reduce the mask's internal volume.

Jacques Mayol considered mask squeeze to be a major problem because the air needed to offset the face-crushing mask limited his maximum depth capability. For vision, he wore scleral contact lenses, which cover the pupils and a large part of the white portion of the eye. Since they have no air space, these lenses made him immune from mask squeeze at any depth.

Because divers who wore snorkels blacked out on the surface while attempting to clear the water, today's record deep freedivers never wear snorkels. Instead, they approach the surface with such force that their bodies literally leap out of the water to waist level where they quickly gulp fresh air.

Techniques vary among deep divers. Many perform personal rituals or are superstitious about how or when they dive. Some meditate, others

Jacques Mayol makes a record attempt (center). At left, he meditates underwater. Above, he demonstrates his scleral contact lenses which eliminate the air space of a face-crushing mask.

practice aggressive hyperventilation and some have been known to throw back a shot of whiskey in preparation for the dive (The latter two practices we certainly do not endorse).

All are stout practitioners of posture and form. They never look down because the tilt of the head, required to see the bottom, causes massive drag. Instead, they look behind while keeping their head and body perfectly inverted. To prevent the disruption of water flow over their bodies, they kick with powerful, narrow strokes, either with their arms tucked along the sides of their bodies or stretched out like a body surfer to prevent the disruption of water flow over their bodies. No-limits divers descend feet-first to facilitate ear equalization and to prevent disorientation.

In 1967, U.S. Navy diver Robert Croft trained to establish a new world depth record for the variable-weight category and became the first man to break the 200-foot barrier (61 meters) in "Project 33 Fathoms Plus." Croft was a trainer at the Submarine Escape Training Tower at the U.S. Naval Base in Groton, Connecticut. At that time, 200 feet was an unthinkable depth because physiologists still believed that an ordinary man would suffer crushed lungs at approximately 161 feet (49 meters). Yet in 1966, off Freeport, Grand Bahama Island, Jacques Mayol had already reached 197 feet (60 meters), proving that the feat was possible for a well-trained, breath-hold diver.

Led by Chief Navy Diver Ernie Colburn, Croft and his team traveled to Fort Lauderdale, Florida, for the record attempt. The first day they set up three descent lines to a depth of 250 feet (76 meters) using 100-pound lead weights at the ends for ballast. Croft, using a 59-pound weight that attached to a hand brake, made practice runs to 135 feet.

Over the next several days, Croft made dives up to 170 feet (52 meters) with no apparent problems. On Sunday, Feb. 5, Croft reached 185 feet, the deepest dive ever made by an American. Foul weather and gear malfunctions hampered further attempts until Ash Wednesday, Feb. 8, 1967, when the weather broke and the seas flattened.

Navy diver John Williams, the safety diver, was placed at 200 feet. Croft began to hyperventilate, filling his almost 8-liter lungs to capacity. Wearing

Mehgan Heaney Grier sets her first record—155 feet (47 meters).

Water Photo: Jim Edds Land Photo: Sixto Nolasco

a shark-skin wetsuit, mask with nose clip and no fins, he began his descent. To alert him of his depth, safety divers tapped Croft as he sped past them. At 217 feet (66 meters), he applied the hand brake, turned toward the surface and, hand-over-hand, made his way back. The dive took 2 minutes and 6 seconds. It was the first time in history that an American had won the record. In 1968, Croft would again regain the record from Jacques Mayol, who in December 1967 descended to 230 feet (70 meters) off Ft. Lauderdale, Florida. Croft would later lose the record to Enzo Maiorca. It would be the last freediving record attempt in any category by an American until 1996, when Mehgan Heaney Grier made her record setting attempt.

When it comes to freediving for depth, no name is more universally known than Jacques Mayol, the guru of apnea and yoga discipline. Mayol has been freediving since the early 1940s and started competing in the mid-1960s. Mayol was the first man to break the 100-meter barrier—a task previously considered impossible. In 1976 off the island of Elba, Italy, Mayol descended to 328 feet (100 meters) in a dive that lasted 3 minutes and 40 seconds. Although he is not well known in the United States, he enjoys a celebrity status around the world, particularly in Europe and Japan, where his book *Homo Delphinus* is a bestseller.

Looking back, Mayol divides his diving career into three phases. The first phase was competitive; this goal was simply to compete for depth and to become world champion. He captured his first title from Tetake Williams of Polynesia in 1966 at the famous Underwater Explorers Society (Unexso) in Freeport, Bahamas. Over the next 10 years, he battled first Croft and then his ultimate rival, Enzo Maiorca.

During his competitive days, Mayol documented strange feelings that could not be explained medically. In an attempt to understand the limits of the human mind and body, he continued diving, even after CMAS halted recognition of such records. It was during this second, experimental phase of his career, in 1981, that Mayol made his deepest dives—331 feet (101 meters) in the no-limits category and 197 feet (60 meters) in the constant-weight category. In 1993, Mayol successfully completed an experimental dive to 344 feet (105 meters), which lasted 3 minutes and 10 seconds. During this phase, Mayol traveled throughout the world allowing scientists to perform various tests on him while he held his breath underwater.

The third phase of Mayol's career includes his present search for the metaphysical elements of man and his relationship with the sea to determine if man has dormant aquatic potential. Mayol also studied man's relationship with marine mammals and started the Homo Delphinus Project, which would bring him back to Unexso to dive with two Atlantic bottlenose dolphins named Bimini and Stripe. If all proceeded as planned, Mayol would simply swim down to 148 feet (45 meters) and summon Bimini and Stripe to pull him back to the surface while he grasped their dorsal fins. It was a risky attempt since no one could predict how the pool-trained dolphins would perform in the open ocean. On Dec. 5, 1993, Mayol's attempt was successful, fulfilling a life-long dream and symbolizing man's close relationship with the sea and its inhabitants.

At the age of 70, although he's no longer engaging in record attempts, Jacques Mayol is still actively diving and out-performing most divers half his age. He is currently writing a new book, a sequel to *Homo Delphinus*—we hope it will be published in English. In the Mayol tradition, Jacques' son, Jean-Jacques, is actively promoting and teaching apnea-diving near his residence in Florida, not far from Mehgan Heaney Grier.

Take a look at the statuesque 19-year-old Mehgan Heaney Grier, and it's easy to guess her occupation—fashion model. Few, however, would single her out as the deepest, constant-weight, breath-hold diver in the United States. Her first record was 155 feet.

What makes her a champion? Mehgan is quick to credit her dive trainer Manny Puig and boyfriend-personal trainer Mark Rackley. But as you talk to her about diving, you sense there's something more than good coaching; it's her love affair with the water.

Mehgan loves what she calls her "secret of the blue"—the feeling of being under the water. "Under your own power, you go to a different place, another dimension," she says. "I like the feeling of water compressing me. I love the blue water—it's so beautiful, so silent."

Mehgan's interest with water began when she learned how to snorkel at age 6, on a Florida vacation away from her land-locked home in Minnesota. At 11, she moved to the Florida Keys, where her ocean-wise stepfather Nelson Grier taught her sea skills, among them how to freedive to 30 feet.

At age 17, on a spearfishing trip to the Marquesses, Mehgan discovered her natural ability for deep diving. Mark introduced her to several freediving techniques, such as hyperventilation and how to keep her descending profile sleek by not looking at the bottom. After giving her his depth-recording watch, Mark advised her not to make any dives deeper than 60 feet (18 meters) deep. Mehgan powered down to 60 feet, where she glanced at the depth gauge and then continued downward. After a minute-and-a-half, Mark and Manny became concerned, until a relaxed Mehgan surfaced. Her depth recorder read 87 feet (27 meters).

That's when the team first realized Mehgan's potential. The two men introduced her to Pipin, who trained her briefly before the team started to practice independently in preparation for the constant-weight record attempt.

Mehgan improved quickly. Soon, on land, she was holding her breath over 4 minutes. In the swimming pool, she swam 300 feet (91 meters) underwater, making energy-sapping turns each 100 feet (30 meters.) The team practiced "drops" in the blue water, where Mehgan discovered her special ability to clear her ears easily at any depth. She trained with weights to strengthen her legs and lungs, sometimes holding her breath to mimic freediving. Packing every breath in deeply, she aimed to increase the air-holding capacity of her lungs.

Bad weather postponed her record attempt several times. When the day finally came, the team discovered the water temperature had plummeted, so they borrowed a wetsuit for Mehgan. It was her first dive with a wetsuit. "It was the best dive I've ever made," she recalls. "At 155 feet (47 meters), I felt good, no pain, no pressure. I felt I could go deeper, but caution told me to turn around early." She made a wise choice because on the way back to the surface, her oversized wetsuit ballooned like a parachute, slowing her ascent rate.

"Mehgan, with her hands clasped at the ends of her outstretched arms, looks like an arrow accelerating straight for the bottom," says photographer Jim Edds.

"I tip over, lean back and arch my back slightly, then shut my eyes," she says. "That position seems to stop the body's natural tendency to fall over. Sometimes, I peep my eyes open a little to glimpse the water rushing by. Depth doesn't seem to have much effect on me. At 80 feet (24 meters), nothing's different. At 100 feet I notice it's slightly harder to clear my ears. Otherwise nothing bothers me—unless I fail to prepare adequately on the surface. I feel good at depth. I actually love the feeling."

There is nothing Mehgan fears about the ocean or her record attempts. She views diving as a big adventure. Even though she dives with hammerhead sharks and Everglades alligators, she stays calm. While she feels that worrying excessively about

risks would hold her back, she is quick to mention the "I'm immortal" mind-set of youth. She advises that anyone practicing for underwater endurance or for depth records proceed with extreme caution, even in a swimming pool, because freedivers often suppress their desire to breathe well past their natural breaking point. "Find a buddy at about your same stage of development," she says. "Alternate practice dives so that each watches out for the other."

About the future, Mehgan suggests that the world's deepest diver may well become a woman. She states that a woman's naturally lower metabolic rate should translate into lower oxygen consumption and, therefore, a deeper dive. "Ultimately, I think that obtaining the record has to do most with the diver's dedication, heart and hunger for the goal."

Recently, Pipin has become a household name in the United States. Living in Florida, he has been setting new no-limits records at least once a year. He has been featured in many dive magazines and television documentaries. David once worked with

Pipin for six months. "He is incredible to watch when he dives," says David. "When you combine his physiological makeup, personal drive, and the fact that he has been continuously diving since he was a child, he's in a class of his own. Besides being a fanatic about hydro-dynamics, he has an ability to equalize like no one I've ever met. Pipin has an enormous 8-liter lung capacity, while the average person (including Mayol) has about 4 liters."

Pipin's current no-limits record stands at 439 feet (134 meters); the feat took place Nov. 26, 1996, in Cabo San Lucas, Mexico. That dive lasted 2 minutes and 22 seconds.

Scientists, physicians and most experts thought that the 100-meter (328-foot) barrier was impossible to surpass. Mayol proved them wrong. Who would ever imagine that the 400-foot (122-meter) mark would be surpassed by two individuals? Will the 500-feet (152-meter) barrier ever be broken? Probably. Pipin says that he will retire when he reaches 500 feet (unless Pellizarri or another diver breaks that record first).

No-limits deep diving records

1991	Pipin	380 feet (116 meters)	Italy
1991	Pellizzari	387 feet (118 meters)	Italy
1992	Pipin	397 feet (121 meters)	Italy
1993	Pellizzari	403 feet (123 meters)	Italy
1993	Pipin	410 feet (125 meters)	Bahamas
1994	Pipin	417 feet (127 meters)	United States
1996	Pipin	439 feet (134 meters)	Mexico

Marine mammals, the ultimate deep divers. Seals
cavort in the surf at Guadalupe Island, Mexico.

APPENDIX I

Freediving resources

DIVE & SAFETY ORGANIZATIONS

Divers Alert Network
3100 Tower Blvd. Suite 1300
Durham, NC 27707
919-684-2948

Underwater Society of America
PO Box 628
Daly City, CA 94017
415-583-8492

MANUFACTURERS AND DISTRIBUTORS OF FREEDIVING EQUIPMENT AND ACCESSORIES

FULL PRODUCT LINE—MASKS, FINS, SNORKELS, WETSUITS, WEIGHT BELTS, KNIVES, FLOATS & FLAGS, SPEARGUNS, STRINGERS, ACCESSORIES.

AB Biller Co.
4 N. Cavalry Dr.
Bloomingdale, IL 60108
630-529-2776

A-Plus Marine
116-B McClure Dr.
Gulf Breeze, FL 32561
904-934-0513

Beuchat USA, Inc.
1321 N.W. 65th Place
Ft. Lauderdale, FL 33309
954-978-1204

Cressi-Sub USA, Inc.
10 Reuten Dr.
Closter, NJ 07624
800-338-9143

Dacor
161 Northfield Rd.
Northfield, IL 60093
708-446-9554

Finis (monofins)
3941 Holly Dr., Suite F
Tracy, Ca. 95376
209-830-2890

Mares
Shore Point, One Selleck St.
Norwalk, CT 06855
800-874-3236

Nemrod
4574 N. Hiatus Rd.
Sunrise, FL 33351
954-572-8668

Omer/Technosport, Inc.
4625 Kincaid Ave.
Norfolk, VA 23502
757-853-2415

Picassosub
2522 Northwest 9th St.
Miami, FL 33125
305-631-0133

ScubaPro
1326 Willow Rd.
Sturtevant, WI 53177
414-884-1662

Team Sports/Esclapez
16704 Hawthorne Blvd.
Lawndale, CA 90260
310-371-8019

U.S. Divers Co., Inc.
3323 West Warner Ave.
Santa Ana, CA 92704
714-540-8010

KAYAKS & DIVE BOARDS— KAYAKS, PADDLES, ANCHORS, BACKRESTS, TETHERS.

Cobra/Glenwa
PO Box 3134
Gardena, CA 90247
310-327-9216

Mendocino
116 Orr Springs Rd.
Ukiah, CA 95482
888-468-9694

Necky Kayaks
1100 Riverside Rd
Abbotsford, British Columbia
V2S 7P1 Canada

Ocean Kayak
PO Box 5003
Ferndale, WA 98248
360-366-4003

SPEARGUNS & SPEARFISHING ACCESSORIES—SPEARGUNS, SHAFTS, SPEAR TIPS, STRINGERS, FLOATS, REELS.

Bandito
94-47 Ukee St.
Waipahu, HI 96797
808-677-7975

Global Mfg. Supply
1829 S. 68th St.
West Allis, WI 53214
414-774-1616

JBL Enterprises
426 W. Almond Ave.
Orange, CA 92666
714-633-0860

National Divers
3420 Yale Way
Fremont, CA 94538
800-729-3483

Riffe International
1030 Calle Sombra #B
San Clemente, CA 92673
714-361-2818

Seabear
2244 East Enterprise
Twinsburg, OH 44087
216-963-3495

Sport Divers Mfg.
1923 N.E. 150th St.
Miami, FL 33181
305-947-5692

Trident Diving Supply
9616 Owensmouth Ave.
Chatsworth, CA 91311
818-998-7518

WETSUITS & WETSUIT ACCESSORIES—DIVE SKINS, HOODS, VESTS, BOOTS, GLOVES.

Body Glove International
530 6th St.
Hermosa Beach, CA 90254
310-374-4074

Deep Thought
5708 Hollister Ave.
Goleta, CA 93117
805-967-4456

Xcel Wetsuits
66-590 Kamehameha Hwy
Haleiwa, HI 96712
808-637-6239

Harvey's
2505 South 252nd St.
Kent, WA 98032
206-824-1114

Henderson Aquatics
301 Orange St.
Millville, NJ 08332
609-825-4771

Sharkskins
1672 15th Street
San Francisco, Ca. 94103-3509
800-957-4275

O'Neil Wetsuits
1071 41st Ave.
Santa Cruz, CA 95063
408-475-7500

Sea Quest
2151 Las Palmas Dr.
Carlsbad, CA 92009
619-438-1101

UNDERWATER PHOTOGRAPHY AND VIDEO EQUIPMENT & ACCESSORIES—CAMERAS, STROBES, HOUSINGS, LENSES.

Amphibico
9563 Cote De Liesse
Dorval, PQH9P1A3 Canada
514-636-9910

Gates Underwater Products
5111 Santa Fe St. Suite H
San Diego, CA 92109
619-272-2501

Ikelite
PO Box 88100
Indianapolis, IN 46208
317-923-4523

Light & Motion Industries
300 Cannery Row
Monterey, CA 93940
408-645-1525

Nikon
1300 Walt Whitman Rd.
Melville, NY 11747
516-547-4392

Sea & Sea
2105 Camino Vida Roble #L
Carlsbad, CA 92009
800-732-7977

Underwater Photo-Tech
16 Manning St. Suite 104
Derry, NH 03038
603-432-1997

APPENDIX II

Glossary

Absolute pressure: The total or true pressure being measured. When underwater, "absolute pressure" refers to the water pressure and atmospheric pressure combined. At sea-level, there is 1 atmosphere of absolute pressure; at 33 feet (10 meters), there are 2 atmospheres of absolute pressure.

Air embolism: A blockage due to an air bubble trapped within the circulatory system. This is a life-threatening event because the air bubble may travel to the heart or brain and block normal circulation. It is caused by the over-expansion of the lungs due to rapid ascents and/or breath-holding ascents by scuba divers or by a physiological anomaly.

Alveoli: Small units in the lungs where gas exchange takes place.

Ama: Woman freedivers in the Orient who earn a living by diving for food such as urchins, abalone, oysters and seaweed.

Antihistamine: A drug that decreases the release of histamine in body tissues. Histamine released in nasal and throat tissue causes swelling, often leading to difficulty in ear clearing. Antihistamines are also frequently used to prevent sea sickness.

Apnea: Absence of breathing. Freedivers are apneic throughout the duration of their dive.

Aperture: The iris or opening of a camera lens, which allows a fixed amount of light to penetrate and expose the film in the camera. Each setting is assigned an **f-stop** number.

Arrythmia: An irregular heartbeat caused by various disturbances such as drugs, breath-holding and forceful **equalizations.** Arrythmias are not uncommon. In certain individuals they might prevent diving, depending upon professional medical evaluation.

Bluewater: Anywhere spearfishers hunt open-ocean gamefish species. It's generally deep, blue and clear but sometimes may be shallow, green and even turbid.

Boyle's law: A law of physics that explains the pressure and volume relationships of gases. It states that a volume of a gas is inversely proportional to the absolute pressure, while the density of that volume of gas is directly proportional. This principle explains how pressure affects air spaces within a diver's body and gear.